No Nonsense
Maths

10–11 years

D0418283

Contents

Central pull-out pages

Calculations

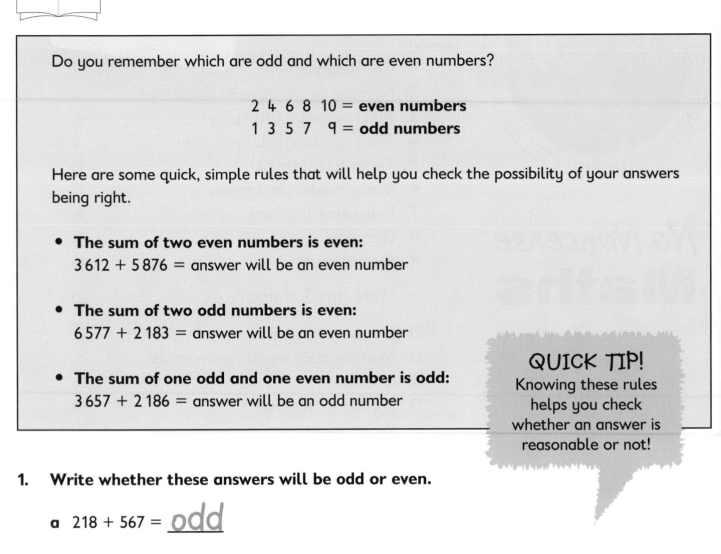

Do you remember which are odd and which are even numbers?

$$2 \ 4 \ 6 \ 8 \ 10 = \textbf{even numbers}$$
$$1 \ 3 \ 5 \ 7 \ \ 9 = \textbf{odd numbers}$$

Here are some quick, simple rules that will help you check the possibility of your answers being right.

- **The sum of two even numbers is even:**
  $3\,612 + 5\,876 =$ answer will be an even number

- **The sum of two odd numbers is even:**
  $6\,577 + 2\,183 =$ answer will be an even number

- **The sum of one odd and one even number is odd:**
  $3\,657 + 2\,186 =$ answer will be an odd number

QUICK TIP!
Knowing these rules helps you check whether an answer is reasonable or not!

1. **Write whether these answers will be odd or even.**

a $218 + 567 = \underline{\text{odd}}$

b $369 + 217 = \underline{\hspace{3em}}$

c $1\,856 + 3\,962 = \underline{\hspace{3em}}$

d $3\,691 + 1\,285 = \underline{\hspace{3em}}$

e $9\,999 + 111 = \underline{\hspace{3em}}$

f $317 + 5\,896 = \underline{\hspace{3em}}$

g $7\,963 + 7\,962 = \underline{\hspace{3em}}$

QUICK TIP!
Again, knowing this can help you check whether an answer is reasonable.

Remember ... there are ways of checking addition, subtraction, multiplication and division number sentences by changing them round.

Look at these.
$587 + 623 = 1\,210 \longrightarrow 1\,210 - 623 = 587$
$381 \times 19 = 7\,239 \longrightarrow 7\,239 \div 381 = 19$

2. **Look at the second column.**
Put a ✓ if the number sentences are correct or a ✗ if they are wrong.

a $217 + 5\,698 = 5\,915$ $5\,915 - 216 = 5\,698$ □

b $27 \times 35 = 945$ $945 \div 27 = 35$ □

c $1035 \div 23 = 45$ $45 \times 24 = 1\,035$ □

d $567 - 278 = 289$ $277 + 289 = 567$ □

e $1289 + 3\,698 = 4\,987$ $4\,987 - 1\,289 = 3\,698$ □

f $1032 \div 12 = 86$ $86 \times 12 = 1\,031$ □

g $7891 - 397 = 7\,494$ $7\,594 + 7\,891 = 387$ □

h $23 \times 23 = 529$ $529 \div 23 = 24$ □

i $7750 \div 125 = 62$ $125 \times 62 = 7\,750$ □

0	Tough	OK	Got it!	15

Total
◺ 15

More practice? Go to www

Challenge yourself

The following number sentences are correct.
Rewrite the number sentences using a different mathematical operation.

a $328 + 567 = 895$ $895 - 567 = 328$

b $72 \times 36 = 2\,592$ _____

c $2296 \div 41 = 56$ _____

d $765 - 389 = 376$ _____

e $3871 + 5\,333 = 9\,204$ _____

f $21 \times 83 = 1\,743$ _____

g $287 - 179 = 108$ _____

Number sequences and properties

Look at these number lines.

Rule: **the numbers decrease 15 at a time**.

231	216	201	186	171	156	141	126	111	96

Rule: **the numbers increase 0.5 at a time**.

1·5	2·0	2·5	3·0	3·5	4·0	4·5	5·0	5·5	6·0

1. **What is the rule for each of these number lines?**

a

208	195	182	169	156	143	130	117	104	91	78

Rule: _____

b

589	564	539	514	489	464	439	414	389	364	339

Rule: _____

c

7·75	7·5	7·25	7	6·75	6·5	6·25	6·0	5·75	5·5	5·25

Rule: _____

2. **Finish these number lines.**

a

−42	−20	2	24	46	68					

b

513	490	467	444	421	398					

c

135	119	103	87	71	55					

d

217	226	235	244	253	262					

There are a few easy rules to help us know whether a whole number is divisible by a certain number. A number is divisible by ...

2 if the last digit is even	132	**3** if the sum of its digits is divisible by 3	168
4 if the last two digits are divisible by 4	112	**5** if the last digit is 0 or 5	435
6 if it is even and also divisible by 3	534	**9** if the sum of its digits is divisible by 9	135
10 if the last digit is 0	890		

3. **Write the number or numbers each of these whole numbers are divisible by.**

a 555 _____

b 356 _____

c 405 _____

d 1010 _____

e 168 _____

f 237 _____

g 356 _____

h 264 _____

i 2 545 _____

j 6 624 _____

4. **How would you know whether a whole number is divisible by 25?**
Write your own rule.

_____

0	Tough	OK	Got it!	18

Total

18

More practice? Go to **www**

Challenge yourself

These number sequences are more challenging. See whether you can finish them, then explain the rule you used.

a

1	1	2	3	5						

Rule: _____

b

1	2	4	8	16						

Rule: _____

c

1	2	5	14	41						

Rule: _____

Addition and subtraction

This is how to do addition calculations using the 'carrying' method ...

2 1 6 **8**	2 1 **6** 8	2 **1** 6 8	**2** 1 6 8
+ 3 9 5 **3**	+ 3 **9** 5 3	+ 3 **9** 5 3	+ 3 **9** 5 3
1	**2** 1	**1** 2 1	**6** 1 2 1
1	1 1	1 1 1	1 1 1

When the numbers in a column total more than 10, the ten is carried to the next column.

1. **Complete these additions.**

a   3 7 6 5
  + 1 6 9 7
  ———

b   7 5 8 9
  + 1 6 6 3
  ———

c   2 7 3 8
  + 3 3 8 5
  ———

d   5 4 7 6
  + 3 7 6 1
  ———

e   1 9 8 3
  + 1 5 6 1
  ———

f   3 2 9 9
  + 1 7 1 6
  ———

g   6 8 1 7
  + 1 6 6 6
  ———

h   2 8 5 6
  + 3 7 7 5
  ———

i   5 9 9 9
  + 2 8 8 8
  ———

2. **Find the total of...**

a 34 568, 128 and 4 458 _____

b £0·78, £2·67 and £32·09 _____

c 45·2, 530·78, 132·0 and 1·52 _____

d 3·6 kg, 267 g, 23·67 kg and 5 g _____

> **QUICK TIP!**
> Remember to line up the units under units, tens under tens etc.

Do you remember how to do subtraction with bigger numbers?
If there are not enough units to take from, change a ten into 10 units.
If there are not enough tens to take from, change a hundred into 10 tens.

Look ...

$$
\begin{array}{r}
3\,6\,7 \\
-\ 1\,6\,9 \\
\hline
\end{array}
\qquad
\begin{array}{r}
3\,{}^{5}6\,{}^{1}7 \\
-\ 1\,6\,9 \\
\hline
8
\end{array}
\qquad
\begin{array}{r}
3\,{}^{5}6\,{}^{1}7 \\
-\ 1\,6\,9 \\
\hline
8
\end{array}
\qquad
\begin{array}{r}
{}^{2}3\,{}^{15}6\,{}^{1}7 \\
-\ 1\,6\,9 \\
\hline
9\,8
\end{array}
\qquad
\begin{array}{r}
{}^{2}3\,{}^{15}6\,{}^{1}7 \\
-\ 1\,6\,9 \\
\hline
1\,9\,8
\end{array}
$$

3. Complete these subtractions.

a
$$
\begin{array}{r}
4\,7\,8 \\
-\ 1\,7\,3 \\
\hline
\\
\hline
\end{array}
$$

b
$$
\begin{array}{r}
2\,6\,0 \\
-\ 1\,8\,7 \\
\hline
\\
\hline
\end{array}
$$

c
$$
\begin{array}{r}
3\,9\,8 \\
-\ 1\,6\,7 \\
\hline
\\
\hline
\end{array}
$$

d
$$
\begin{array}{r}
5\,6\,8 \\
-\ 2\,2\,9 \\
\hline
\\
\hline
\end{array}
$$

e
$$
\begin{array}{r}
6\,7\,5 \\
-\ 2\,8\,8 \\
\hline
\\
\hline
\end{array}
$$

f
$$
\begin{array}{r}
3\,2\,9 \\
-\ 1\,9\,7 \\
\hline
\\
\hline
\end{array}
$$

0			19
Tough	OK	Got it!	

Total
19

More practice? Go to 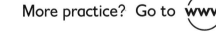 www

Challenge yourself

Find the difference between ...

a 8 253 and 517   _____

b £3·28 and £1·75   _____

c 751·6 and 283·2   _____

d 3·3 l and 230 ml   _____

QUICK TIP!
Again, remember to line up the units under units and tens under tens etc.

7

Lesson 4

Short and long multiplication

Do you remember?	2 6
	× 6
	1 2 0 (20 × 6)
	3 6 (6 × 6)
	1 5 6 (26 × 6)

1. Find the answers.

a
```
    5 6
×     2
_____

_____
```

b
```
    7 8
×     5
_____

_____
```

c
```
    3 2
×     6
_____

_____
```

d
```
  2 7 1
×     7
_____

_____
```

e
```
  1 6 3
×     6
_____

_____
```

f
```
  2 2 1
×     7
_____

_____
```

Look at how we do long multiplication.

```
      2 6 5
×       2 2
_____
    5 3 0 0  (265 × 20)
      5 3 0  (265 × 2)
_____
    5 8 3 0  (265 × 22)
```

It is very similar to the multiplication problems we have already done.

2. Complete these multiplications.

a
```
    4 2 2
×     2 3
_____
            (422 × 20)
_____
            (422 × 3)
_____
            (422 × 23)
```

b
```
    5 2 1
×     2 7
_____
            (521 × 20)
_____
            (521 × 7)
_____
            (521 × 27)
```

c   1 5 1
  ×   3 1
  ───────

  ───────

d   2 0 2
  ×   3 4
  ───────

  ───────

e   2 3 5
  ×   4 1
  ───────

  ───────

f   3 5 1
  ×   5 1
  ───────

  ───────

			Total
0 Tough	OK	Got it! 12	12

More practice? Go to www

Challenge yourself

Solve these problems.

a A box contains 235 ice-lollies.
How many ice-lollies will be in 26 boxes? _____

b Cleo the cat eats 42 cans of cat food a month. A can of cat food costs 32p.
How much does Cleo's food cost for a month? _____

c A football sticker book holds 135 stickers.
How many stickers will 25 books hold? _____

Times tables to 10

1. **How quickly can you answer these multiplication questions?**

Time yourself. Can you do them all in 30 seconds?

$3 \times 6 =$ _____ $7 \times 7 =$ _____

$8 \times 7 =$ _____ $2 \times 8 =$ _____

$9 \times 2 =$ _____ $9 \times 6 =$ _____

$6 \times 6 =$ _____ $7 \times 6 =$ _____

$7 \times 3 =$ _____ $3 \times 3 =$ _____

$5 \times 9 =$ _____ $5 \times 8 =$ _____

$10 \times 8 =$ _____ $6 \times 9 =$ _____

$6 \times 4 =$ _____ $10 \times 4 =$ _____

$3 \times 9 =$ _____ $8 \times 8 =$ _____

$8 \times 6 =$ _____ $9 \times 0 =$ _____

$7 \times 5 =$ _____ $2 \times 7 =$ _____

$9 \times 9 =$ _____ $5 \times 5 =$ _____

$8 \times 3 =$ _____ $4 \times 7 =$ _____

$2 \times 2 =$ _____ $10 \times 10 =$ _____

$5 \times 10 =$ _____ $1 \times 1 =$ _____

$3 \times 4 =$ _____ $6 \times 5 =$ _____

QUICK TIP!
If you write the answers in pencil you can rub them out and have another go to try to beat your time.

1st attempt ...
How long did it take you? _____ seconds

2nd attempt ...
How long did it take you? _____ seconds

3rd attempt ...
How long did it take you? _____ seconds

2. **Answer these questions.**

a What are five nines? _____

b What is 8 times 8? _____

c What is 3 multiplied by 7? _____

d What is 4 times 8? _____

e Multiply seven by nine. _____

f What are six sixes? _____

g What is 10 multiplied by 6? _____

h What are five eights? _____

i What is 7 multiplied by 8? _____

j Multiply two by nine. _____

k What is four multiplied by four? _____

l Multiply 8 by 6. _____

3. **Fill in the boxes.**

a 6 × ☐ = 30

b ☐ × 5 = 45

c ☐ × 9 = 18

d 7 × ☐ = 56

e ☐ × 6 = 42

f 4 × ☐ = 32

g ☐ × 7 = 70

h ☐ × 6 = 48

i 3 × ☐ = 24

j ☐ × 9 = 27

k 9 × ☐ = 81

l ☐ × 10 = 100

			Total
0 Tough	OK	Got it! 25	25

More practice? Go to www

Challenge yourself

Complete the number sentences.

a ☐ × ☐ = 24

b ☐ × ☐ = 54

c ☐ × ☐ = 48

d ☐ × ☐ = 49

e ☐ × ☐ = 2

f ☐ × ☐ = 72

g ☐ × ☐ = 36

h ☐ × ☐ = 18

i ☐ × ☐ = 9

j ☐ × ☐ = 63

Mode, median and mean

To find the mode or median
This set of numbers needs to be put in order from smallest to largest.

2   6   3   5   8   6   1   6   7   3   4

This is the same set of numbers in order.

1   2   3   3   4   5   (6   6   6)   7   8
                              ↑

Mode = the number that appears the **most times** = **6**
Median = the number that is in the **middle** of the list = **5**

1. **Find the mode and median of these numbers.**
   Remember to put the numbers in order first.

   a   2   3   8   7   3   6   5   3   6

       2   3   3   3   5   6   6   7   8

       Mode = _____   Median = _____

   b   7   1   6   1   4   3   2   1   6

       ____ ____ ____ ____ ____ ____ ____ ____ ____

       Mode = _____   Median = _____

   c   2   5   6   7   2   5   9   3   2

       ____ ____ ____ ____ ____ ____ ____ ____ ____

       Mode = _____   Median = _____

2. **These are the heights in centimetres of 11 children.**
   Find the mode and median.

   137   129   138   136   131   136   131   132   131   139   133

   129 131 ____ ____ ____ ____ ____ ____ ____ ____ ____

   Mode = _____   Median = _____

To find the **mean** of a set of numbers: 2 6 8 3 1 2 6

1 Find the **total** of the numbers: 2 + 6 + 8 + 3 + 1 + 2 + 6 = **28**
2 Count how many numbers are in the set = **7**
3 Divide the total by the number of numbers in the set: **28 ÷ 7 = 4**

The **mean** (or average) is **4**.

3. **Below are the shoe sizes of eight 11-year-olds.**

What is their mean shoe size? _____

3   4   5   3   4   4   2   7

4. **Below are the weights of five 11-year-olds.**

What is their mean weight? _____ kg

45 kg   39 kg   46 kg   42 kg   43 kg

0 Tough	OK	Got it! 6

Total

6

More practice? Go to www

Challenge yourself

Ask someone to choose 21 numbers at random between 1 and 10.
Write them in the box below.

QUICK TIP!
You might need a
calculator to help you
find the mean of the
numbers!

Find the mode, median and mean of the numbers.

Mode = _____   Median = _____   Mean = _____

Equivalent fractions

The same fraction can be written in a number of ways.

$$\frac{1}{3} \qquad \frac{2}{6} \qquad \frac{3}{9} \qquad \frac{4}{12}$$

Look carefully at these fractions.

$\frac{1}{3}$ $\frac{2}{6}$ $\frac{3}{9}$ $\frac{4}{12}$ **are all the same size**, or **equivalent** to each other.

They are called **equivalent fractions**.
Notice how the numerator and the denominator are
multiplied by the same number to find an equivalent fraction.

QUICK TIP!

$\frac{1}{3}$ ← numerator
$\phantom{\frac{1}{3}}$ ← denominator.

1. **Write the equivalent fractions.**

a $\frac{1}{4}$ $\frac{2}{8}$ $\frac{3}{12}$ $\frac{4}{16}$ $\frac{5}{20}$ $\frac{6}{24}$

b $\frac{1}{2}$ $\frac{2}{}$ $\frac{3}{}$ $\frac{4}{}$ $\frac{5}{}$ $\frac{6}{}$

c $\frac{1}{5}$ $\frac{2}{}$ $\frac{}{}$ $\frac{}{}$ $\frac{}{}$ $\frac{}{}$

d $\frac{1}{6}$

e $\frac{1}{10}$

$\frac{14}{4} = 3\frac{1}{2}$

There are 14 quarters in $3\frac{1}{2}$.

2. Change these improper fractions into mixed numbers.

a $\frac{17}{5} = 3\frac{2}{5}$

b $\frac{16}{3} = 5\frac{1}{3}$

c $\frac{21}{4} =$ ____

d $\frac{46}{9} =$ ____

e $\frac{30}{7} =$ ____

f $\frac{17}{2} =$ ____

g $\frac{36}{9} =$ ____

h $\frac{25}{8} =$ ____

3. Write three more fractions that are equivalent to ...

a $\frac{9}{12}$ ____ ____ ____

b $\frac{2}{7}$ ____ ____ ____

c $\frac{1}{1}$ ____ ____ ____

d $\frac{11}{10}$ ____ ____ ____

e $\frac{40}{100}$ ____ ____ ____

f $\frac{24}{48}$ ____ ____ ____

4. Complete the fractions.

a $\frac{5}{} = \frac{1}{4}$

b $\frac{20}{100} = \frac{}{5}$

c $\frac{18}{24} = \frac{3}{}$

d $\frac{}{16} = 1\frac{1}{8}$

0			21
Tough	OK	Got it!	

Total

21 / 21

More practice? Go to www

Challenge yourself

Name the smallest equivalent fraction...

a that is three times as much as two-eighths. _____

b that is half of ten-twentieths. _____

c that is the same as thirteen-hundredths. _____

d that is two times four twenty-fourths. _____

Decimals

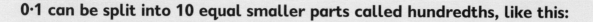

Decimals are numbers that are, or include amounts that are, less than 1.

$2·3 = 2$ units and 3 tenths $= 2\frac{3}{10}$

0·1 can be split into 10 equal smaller parts called hundredths, like this:

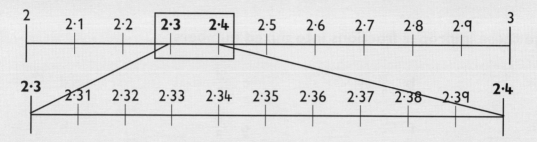

$2·36 = 2$ units, 3 tenths and 6 hundredths $= 2\frac{36}{100}$

0·01 can be split into 10 equal smaller parts called thousandths.

$2·364 = 2$ units, 3 tenths, 6 hundredths and 4 thousandths $= 2\frac{364}{1000}$

---

1. **Match the written number with the correct card. Join the dots.**

   a Eight units, three tenths and two hundredths   •   • 13·19

   b Two units, six tenths and one thousandth   •   • 6·054

   c Thirteen units, one tenth and nine hundredths   •   • 5·55

   d Six units, five hundredths and four thousandths   •   • 2·601

   e Twenty-two units, eight tenths and one hundredth   •   • 8·32

   f Five units, five tenths and five hundredths   •   • 22·81

2. **Continue these patterns.**

   a

3·26	3·28	3·30	3·32				

   b

4·65	4·70	4·75					5·00

3. **Place these decimals on the number line.**

Use arrows to show where they go.

10·89   10·99   11·16

```
        10·9              11·0              11·1              11·2
      +-|-+-+-+-+-+-+-+-+-|-+-+-+-+-+-+-+-+-|-+-+-+-+-+-+-+-+-|-+-+
```

4. **Round to the nearest whole number.**

a 9·65 _____   9·38 _____   9·55 _____

b 10·8 _____   10·5 _____   10·1 _____

c 7·198 _____   7·318 _____   7·678 _____

d 56·89 _____   56·98 _____   56·09 _____

5. **Write the following to one decimal place.**

a 6·72 _____   b 3·98 _____   c 4·44 _____

d 9·761 _____   e 2·232 _____   f 5·555 _____

0 Tough	OK	Got it!	19

Total

19 / 19

More practice? Go to **www**

Challenge yourself

Place these decimals in order, largest first.

a 12·3   13·21   12·212   13·2   12·32   12·232

_____   _____   _____   _____   _____   _____

b 5·55   5·5   50·055   50·505   0·5   55·5

_____   _____   _____   _____   _____   _____

Co-ordinates

Co-ordinates allow us to find an exact place on a grid.

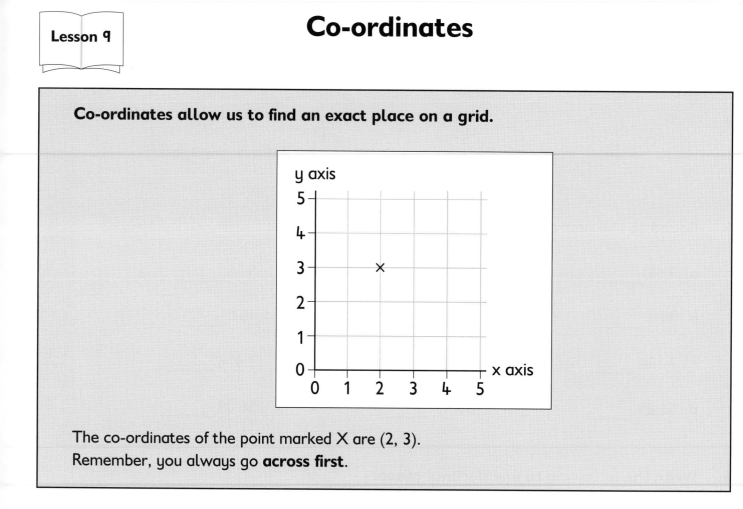

The co-ordinates of the point marked X are (2, 3).
Remember, you always go **across first**.

1. **Place neat crosses on this grid for the co-ordinates listed.**

(8, 9)
(10, 7)
(10, 3)
(8, 1)
(4, 1)
(2, 3)
(2, 7)
(4, 9)

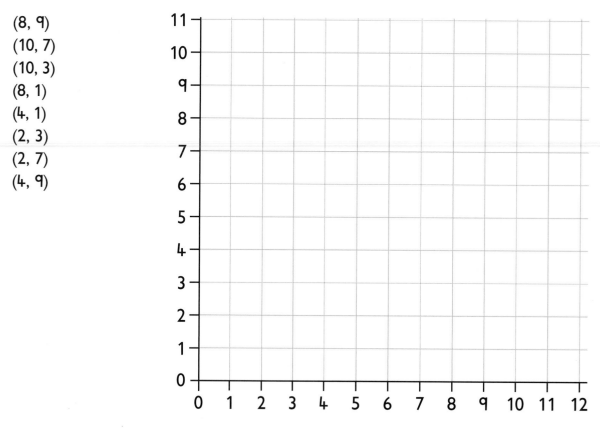

Neatly join the crosses in order.

What shape have you drawn? _____

18

This grid shows clearly the **x-axis** and **y-axis**.
It is divided into four **quadrants**.

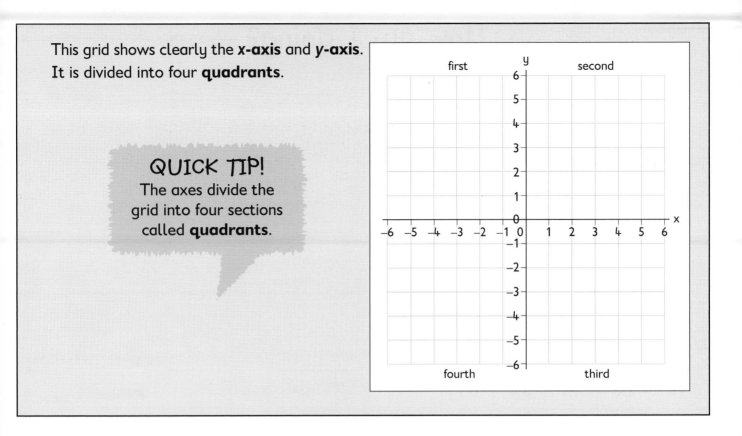

QUICK TIP!
The axes divide the
grid into four sections
called **quadrants**.

2. **Write the co-ordinates of a rectangle using the grid above.**
Each vertex should be in a different quadrant!

_____ _____ _____ _____

0	Tough	OK	Got it!

2

Total

2

More practice? Go to www

Challenge yourself

Write the co-ordinates of the square if it
were reflected in the *x*-axis.

a _____ _____

_____ _____

Write the co-ordinates of the square if it
were reflected in the *y*-axis.

b _____ _____

_____ _____

19

1. **Will the answers be odd or even?**

   a 369 + 217 = _____

   b 892 + 586 = _____

   c 674 + 233 = _____

   d 567 + 341 = _____

2. **Continue the number sequences.**

   a

2·8	4·1	5·4	6·7				

   b

156	139	122	105				

3. **Add or subtract...**

   a
   ```
     6237
   + 1378
   ──────

   ──────
   ```

   b
   ```
     1726
   + 3391
   ──────

   ──────
   ```

   c
   ```
     369
   − 153
   ─────

   ─────
   ```

   d
   ```
     736
   − 285
   ─────

   ─────
   ```

4. **Multiply...**

   a
   ```
     125
   ×  16
   ─────


   ─────

   ─────
   ```

   b
   ```
     334
   ×  21
   ─────


   ─────

   ─────
   ```

   c
   ```
     125
   ×  16
   ─────


   ─────

   ─────
   ```

5. **a** $7 \times 3 =$ _____

   b $8 \times$ _____ $= 56$

   c _____ $\times 4 = 24$

   d $7 \times 9 =$ _____

   e $5 \times$ _____ $= 25$

   f $4 \times$ _____ $= 16$

   g $6 \times$ _____ $= 54$

   h _____ $\times 6 = 48$

   i $9 \times$ _____ $= 81$

6. **Find the mean of these numbers.**

   a 7 4 5 8 2 4   Mean = _____

   b 2 6 7 12 8   Mean = _____

7. **Write the equivalent fractions.**

   a $\frac{1}{2}$ $\frac{2}{}$ ___ $\frac{}{8}$ ___   ___

   b $\frac{1}{5}$ ___   ___ $\frac{}{20}$ $\frac{5}{}$ ___

   c $\frac{1}{3}$ ___   ___   ___   ___   ___

8. **Round these decimals to the nearest whole number.**

   a 45.67 _____   **b** 7.823 _____   **c** 215.455 _____

9. **Write the co-ordinates of the vertices of this square.**

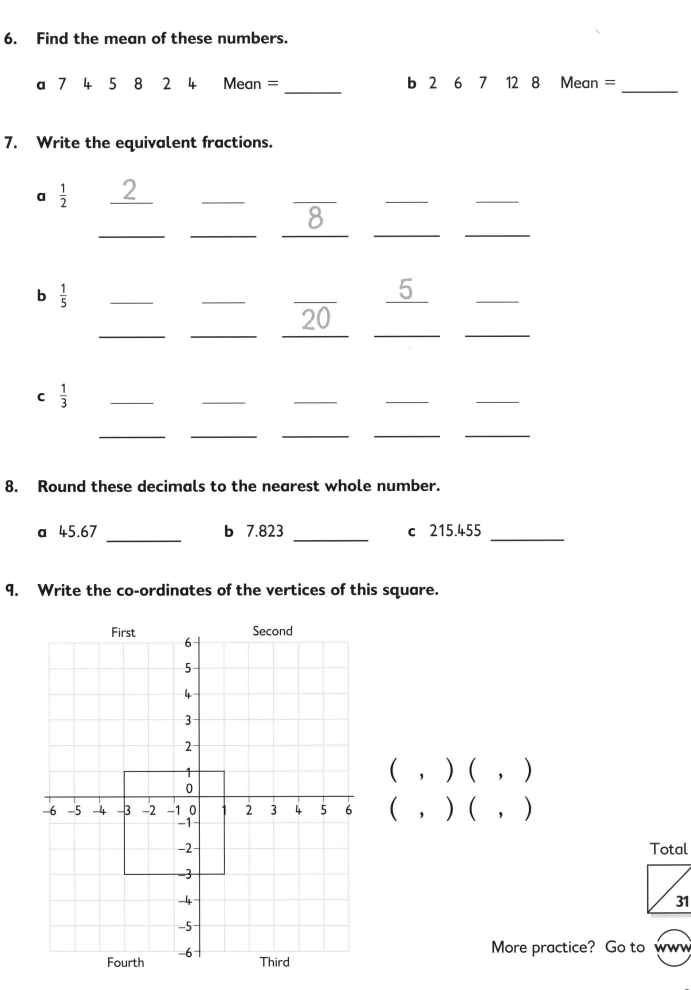

   (,) (,)

   (,) (,)

Total

31

More practice? Go to www

Negative numbers

−10	−9	−8	−7	−6	−5	−4	−3	−2	−1	0	1	2	3	4	5	6	7	8	9	10

← negative numbers →← positive numbers →

1. **Put these integers in order, smallest first.**

a   7   −8   5   −1   −3   6

     −8   −3   −1   5   6   7

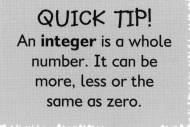

QUICK TIP!
An **integer** is a whole number. It can be more, less or the same as zero.

b   −15   20   33   −18   2   5

____   ____   ____   ____   ____   ____

c   12   2   −12   0   1   −2

____   ____   ____   ____   ____   ____

d   −28   −36   −54   −12   −14   −21

____   ____   ____   ____   ____   ____

e   21   −1   31   −5   −14   16

____   ____   ____   ____   ____   ____

f   −3   30   33   −300   −303   −30

____   ____   ____   ____   ____   ____

g   62   21   −14   38   61   −7

____   ____   ____   ____   ____   ____

2. Solve these problems.

a The temperature is −2°C. It rises by 6°C.

What is the temperature now? _____ °C.

b The temperature is −8°C. It rises by 8°C.

What is the temperature now? _____ °C.

c The temperature is −5°C.

How much does it rise to reach 10°C? _____

d The temperature is −20°C.

How much does it rise to reach 1°C? _____

e The temperature is −15°C. It rises by 7°C.

What is the temperature now? _____

f The temperature is −6°C.

How much does it rise to reach 23°C? _____

0			12
Tough	OK	Got it!	

Total

12 / 12

More practice? Go to www

More practice? Go to www

Challenge yourself

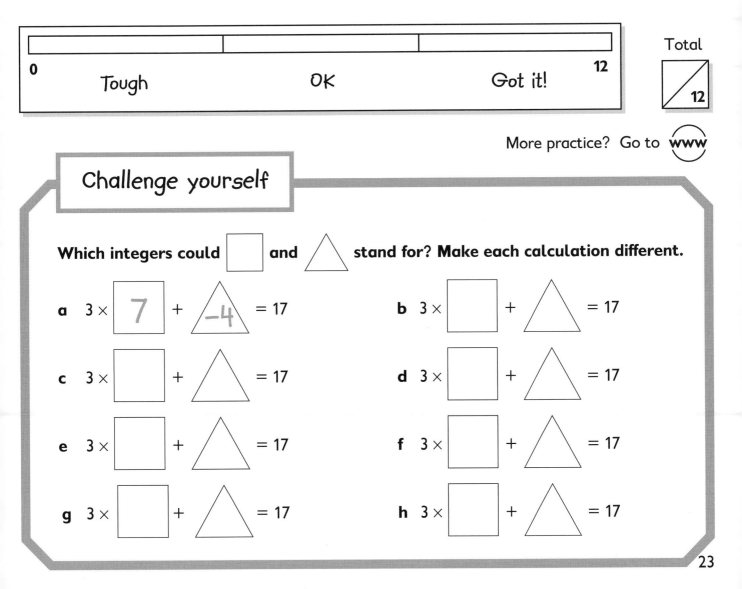

Which integers could ☐ **and** △ **stand for? Make each calculation different.**

a 3 × [7] + /−4\ = 17

b 3 × ☐ + △ = 17

c 3 × ☐ + △ = 17

d 3 × ☐ + △ = 17

e 3 × ☐ + △ = 17

f 3 × ☐ + △ = 17

g 3 × ☐ + △ = 17

h 3 × ☐ + △ = 17

23

Multiplication involving decimals

When multiplying decimals, it is a good idea to make an approximation of the answer first.

$5.2 \times 4 = ?$ 5.2×4 is approximately 5×4 which equals 20.

So the answer should be close to 20.

$$5.2 \times 4 \quad (5.0 \times 4) = 20.0$$
$$(0.2 \times 4) = 0.8$$
$$\overline{20.8}$$

QUICK TIP!
Remember, the decimal points must always line up under each other.

1. **Write the approximate answer to these multiplication number sentences.**

   a $6.1 \times 7 = ?$ $6 \times 7 = 42$

   b $3.9 \times 4 = ?$ _____

   c $2.7 \times 8 = ?$ _____

   d $5.8 \times 2 = ?$ _____

   e $9.9 \times 6 = ?$ _____

   f $1.4 \times 9 = ?$ _____

2. **Find the answers.**

   a 4.9×4 (____ × ____) = _____

   (____ × ____) = _____

   _____

   b 7.1×8 (____ × ____) = _____

   (____ × ____) = _____

   _____

   c 3.6×2 (____ × ____) = _____

   (____ × ____) = _____

   _____

   d 5.8×7 (____ × ____) = _____

   (____ × ____) = _____

   _____

   e 1.9×9 (____ × ____) = _____

   (____ × ____) = _____

   _____

   f 3.5×6 (____ × ____) = _____

   (____ × ____) = _____

   _____

3. **Complete these number sentences.**

   a $5.9 \times 2 =$ _____

   b $6.6 \times 6 =$ _____

   c $3.4 \times 9 =$ _____

This is how to multiply decimals to two decimal points.

5·23 × 4 = ?   5·23 × 4 is approximately 5 × 4 which equals 20.

Again, the answer should be close to 20.

$$5·23 × 4 \quad (5·00 × 4) = 20·00$$
$$(0·20 × 4) = 0·80$$
$$(0·03 × 4) = 0·12$$
$$\overline{20·92}$$

4. **Fill the gaps.**

a   3·21 × 4 (_____ × _____) = _____

(_____ × _____) = _____

(_____ × _____) = _____

_____

b   6·19 × 5 (_____ × _____) = _____

(_____ × _____) = _____

(_____ × _____) = _____

_____

c   4·67 × 3 (_____ × _____) = _____

(_____ × _____) = _____

(_____ × _____) = _____

_____

d   2·18 × 6 (_____ × _____) = _____

(_____ × _____) = _____

(_____ × _____) = _____

_____

0			18
Tough	OK	Got it!	

Total

18

More practice? Go to **www**

Challenge yourself

Solve the problems.

£9·75

a   Crudwell football team needs to replace five of its football shirts.
Each new shirt will cost £9.75.
How much will it cost to replace all five football shirts? _____

b   For Annabel's birthday treat she has invited eight friends to visit the zoo.
It costs £5.30 plus 45p for some food to feed the animals, for each child.
How much does it cost for Annabel and her friends to visit the zoo and feed
the animals? _____

Division

Do you remember?
We divide large numbers like this …

$189 \div 9$ $9\overline{)189}$

How many 9s in 1? 0 r1 $9\overline{)1^189}$

How many 9s in 18? 2   **2**
                                    $9\overline{)1^189}$

How many 9s in 9? 1   **2 1**
                                    $9\overline{)189}$

$189 \div 9 = 21$

1. **Divide …**

a $5\overline{)255}$ **b** $7\overline{)714}$

c $6\overline{)366}$ **d** $4\overline{)648}$

e $3\overline{)429}$ **f** $5\overline{)156}$

g $8\overline{)249}$ **h** $7\overline{)499}$

i $4\overline{)328}$ **j** $5\overline{)359}$

k $6\overline{)547}$ **l** $2\overline{)187}$

m $8\overline{)248}$ **n** $9\overline{)219}$

QUICK TIP!
Watch out! Some of these answers have remainders!

Look carefully at this.

$843 \div 28$ $28\overline{)8\ 43}$

How many 28s in 8? 0 r8 $28\overline{)8\,^{8}43}$

$$\begin{array}{r} 3 \\ 28\overline{)8\,^{8}43} \end{array}$$

How many 28s in 84? 3

$$\begin{array}{r} \mathbf{30\ r3} \\ 28\overline{)8\,^{8}43} \end{array}$$

How many 28s in 3? 0 or 3

$843 \div 28 = 30\ r3$

2. **Divide ...**

a $36\overline{)725}$

b $21\overline{)847}$

c $46\overline{)929}$

0			17
Tough	OK	Got it!	

Total

17

More practice? Go to www

Challenge yourself

Solve these problems.

a   A class of 22 children were given a jar of 887 sweets (lucky them!).
How many sweets did they get each? _____

b   680 children go to Newport Primary School.
There is an average of 34 children in each class.
How many classes are there? _____

Fractions of numbers

There are four quarters in 1 whole.

If you want to find $\frac{1}{4}$ of a number you need to understand that $\frac{1}{4}$ is the same as dividing by 4.

$\frac{1}{4}$ of 20 is the same as 20 ÷ 4

So... $\frac{1}{4}$ of 20 = 5

1. **Answer the following questions.**

   a How many halves in 2? _____

   b How many quarters in $2\frac{1}{4}$? _____

   c How many halves in $4\frac{1}{2}$? _____

   d How many thirds in 1? _____

   e How many quarters in $5\frac{1}{2}$? _____

   f How many thirds in $2\frac{1}{3}$? _____

   g How many quarters in $3\frac{3}{4}$? _____

   h How many thirds in $3\frac{2}{3}$? _____

2. **What is...**

   a $\frac{1}{2}$ of 24? _____   **b** $\frac{1}{4}$ of 20? _____

   c $\frac{1}{3}$ of 18? _____   **d** $\frac{1}{9}$ of 45? _____

   e $\frac{1}{10}$ of 100? _____   **f** $\frac{1}{5}$ of 35? _____

   g $\frac{1}{4}$ of 16? _____   **h** $\frac{1}{2}$ of 46? _____

   i $\frac{1}{6}$ of 54? _____   **j** $\frac{1}{8}$ of 64? _____

3. **Find...**

a $\frac{2}{5}$ of   25 _____   50 _____   100 _____

QUICK TIP!

If $\frac{1}{5}$ of 10 = 2 then

$\frac{2}{5}$ of 10 = 4

b $\frac{3}{4}$ of   24 _____   80 _____   120 _____

c $\frac{3}{10}$ of   30 _____   100 _____   150 _____

d $\frac{2}{7}$ of   70 _____   49 _____   77 _____

e $\frac{4}{5}$ of   50 _____   30 _____   60 _____

4. **What fraction of...**

a £1.00 is 60p? _____   b 1 kg is 250 g? _____

c 1 cm is 3 mm? _____   d 1 l is 500 ml? _____

e £1.50 is 50p? _____   f 3 kg is 1000 g? _____

g 1 m is 89 cm? _____   h 2 l is 20 ml? _____

0			31
Tough	OK	Got it!	

Total

/

31

More practice? Go to www

Challenge yourself

What fraction of a day is...

a   8 hours of sleep? _____

b   1 hour of lunchtime? _____

c   3 hours playing on bikes with friends? _____

d   one minute? _____

29

Percentages

Percentages are a way of dividing whole numbers into hundredths.

A percentage is the number of parts in every 100.

century = 100 years
per cent = in every 100
1 per cent = 1 in every 100
50 per cent = 50 in every 100

QUICK TIP!
% is the sign for **per cent**.

1 per cent can be written as $\frac{1}{100}$ or **1%**

50 per cent can be written as $\frac{50}{100}$ or **50%**

---

1. Look at this table.

Fraction	Decimal	Percentage
1	1.0	100%
$\frac{1}{2}$	0.5	50%
$\frac{1}{4}$	0.25	25%
$\frac{1}{10}$	0.1	10%
$\frac{1}{100}$	0.01	1%

QUICK TIP!
Don't forget to write the percentage sign.

Write the percentage that is the same as these fractions and decimals.

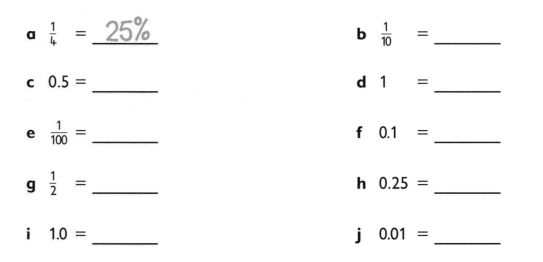

a $\frac{1}{4}$ = _25%_

b $\frac{1}{10}$ = _____

c 0.5 = _____

d 1 = _____

e $\frac{1}{100}$ = _____

f 0.1 = _____

g $\frac{1}{2}$ = _____

h 0.25 = _____

i 1.0 = _____

j 0.01 = _____

If $\frac{1}{10}$ = 10% $\frac{8}{10}$ = 8 × 10% = 80%

If $\frac{1}{4}$ = 25% $\frac{3}{4}$ = 3 × 25% = 75%

2. Write the percentages for the following fractions.

a $\frac{2}{10}$ = _20%_

b $\frac{1}{2}$ = _____

c $\frac{6}{100}$ = _____

d $\frac{2}{4}$ = _____

e $\frac{7}{10}$ = _____

f $\frac{89}{100}$ = _____

g $\frac{46}{100}$ = _____

h $\frac{2}{2}$ = _____

i $\frac{23}{100}$ = _____

3. What percentage of the shape below is shaded?

a _50%_

b _____

c _____

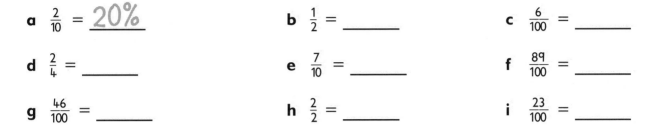

4. Colour in the correct percentage on these shapes.

a 20%

b 75%

c 70%

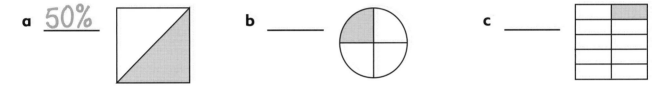

| 0 | Tough | OK | Got it! | 22 |

Total

22 / 22

More practice? Go to www

Challenge yourself

Find ...

a 50% of £100 = _£50_

b 10% of £100 = _____

c 70% of 100 cm = _____

d 20% of 100 books = _____

e 1% of 100p = _____

f 50% of £60 = _____

g 25% of £60 = _____

h 10% of 50 cm = _____

i 75% of 80 m = _____

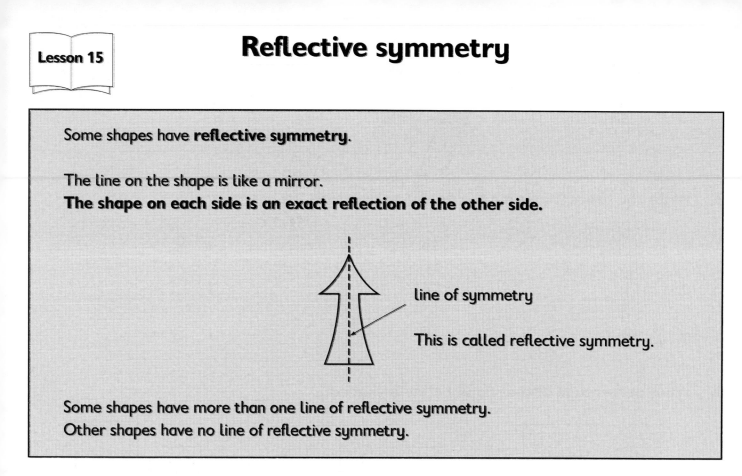

Reflective symmetry

Some shapes have **reflective symmetry**.

The line on the shape is like a mirror.
The shape on each side is an exact reflection of the other side.

line of symmetry

This is called reflective symmetry.

Some shapes have more than one line of reflective symmetry.
Other shapes have no line of reflective symmetry.

1. **Look at these shapes and write how many lines of reflective symmetry they have.**
   If it helps, draw the lines of symmetry on each shape.

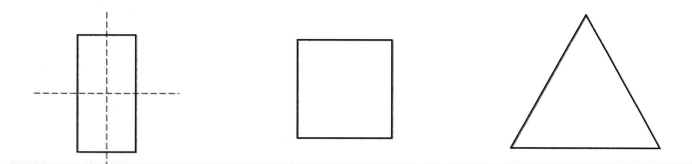

a __2__   b _____   c _____

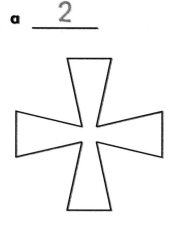 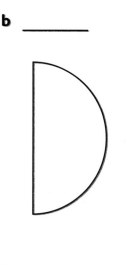 

d _____   e _____   f _____

No Nonsense
Maths

10-11
years

Parents' notes

What your child will learn from this book

Bond No Nonsense will help your child to understand and become more confident in their maths work. This book features all the main maths objectives covered by your child's class teacher during the school year. It provides clear, straightforward teaching and learning of the essentials in a rigorous, step-by-step way.

How you can help

Following a few simple guidelines will ensure that your child gets the best from this book:

- Explain that the book will help your child become confident in their maths work.
- If your child has difficulty reading the text on the page or understanding a question, do provide help.
- Provide scrap paper to give your child extra space for rough working.
- Encourage your child to complete all the exercises in a lesson. You can mark the work using this answer section (which you will also find on the website). Your child can record their own impressions of the work using the 'How did I do' feature.

0			19
	Tough	OK	Got it!

- The 'How am I doing?' sections provide a further review of progress.

Using the website – www.bondlearning.co.uk

- The website provides extra practice of every skill in the book. So if your child does not feel confident about a lesson, they can go to the website and have another go.
- For every page of this book you will find further practice questions and their answers available to download.
- To access the extra practice pages:
  1. Go to www.bondlearning.co.uk
  2. Click on 'Maths'.
  3. Click on '10-11 years'.
  4. Click on the lesson you want.

Bond No Nonsense 10–11 years Answers

① Calculations p2
1   **b** even   **c** even   **d** even   **e** even   **f** odd   **g** odd
2   **a** ✗   **b** ✓   **c** ✗   **d** ✗   **e** ✓   **f** ✗   **g** ✗   **h** ✗   **i** ✓

Challenge yourself
b $2\,592 \div 72 = 36$ or $2\,592 \div 36 = 72$ **c** $41 \times 56 = 2\,296$
d $389 + 376 = 765$
e $9\,204 - 3\,871 = 5\,333$ or $9\,204 - 5\,333 = 3\,871$
f $1\,743 \div 21 = 83$ or $1\,743 \div 83 = 21$ **g** $179 + 108 = 287$

② Number sequences and properties p4
1   **a** the numbers decrease 13 at a time
    b the numbers decrease 25 at a time
    c the numbers decrease 0·25 at a time
2   **a** 90, 112, 134, 156, 178   **b** 375, 352, 329, 306, 283
    c 39, 23, 7, −9, −25   **d** 271, 280, 289, 298, 307
3   **a** 3, 5   **b** 2, 4   **c** 3, 5, 9   **d** 2, 5, 10   **e** 2, 3, 4, 6, 7
    f 3   **g** 2, 4   **h** 2, 3, 4, 6, 11, 12   **i** 5   **j** 2, 3, 4, 6, 8, 9
4   The last two digits would have to be 00, 25, 50 or 75.

Challenge yourself
a   8, 13, 21, 34, 55; Add together the last two numbers
b   32, 64, 128, 256, 512; Double the last number
c   122, 365, 1 094, 3 281, 9 842; Multiply the last number by 3 and take away 1 (or equivalent)

③ Addition and subtraction p6
1   **a** 5 462   **b** 9 252   **c** 6 123   **d** 9 237   **e** 3 544
    f 5 015   **g** 8 483   **h** 6 631   **i** 8 887
2   **a** 39 154   **b** £35·54   **c** 709·5   **c** 27·542 kg
3   **a** 305   **b** 73   **c** 231   **d** 339   **e** 387   **f** 132

Challenge yourself
a 7 736   **b** £1·53   **c** 468·4   **d** 3·07l

④ Short and long multiplication p8
1   **a** 112   **b** 390   **c** 192   **d** 1897   **e** 978   **f** 1547

2   **a**
$$\begin{array}{r} 422 \\ \times\ 23 \\ \hline 8\,440\ (422 \times 20) \\ 1\,266\ (422 \times\ \ 3) \\ \hline 9\,706 \end{array}$$
  b
$$\begin{array}{r} 521 \\ \times\ 27 \\ \hline 10\,420\ (521 \times 20) \\ 3\,647\ (521 \times\ \ 7) \\ \hline 14\,067 \end{array}$$
  c
$$\begin{array}{r} 151 \\ \times\ 31 \\ \hline 4\,530\ (151 \times 30) \\ 151\ (151 \times\ \ 1) \\ \hline 4\,681 \end{array}$$

    d
$$\begin{array}{r} 202 \\ \times\ 34 \\ \hline 6\,060\ (202 \times 30) \\ 808\ (202 \times\ \ 4) \\ \hline 6\,868 \end{array}$$
  e
$$\begin{array}{r} 235 \\ \times\ 41 \\ \hline 9\,400\ (235 \times 40) \\ 235\ (235 \times\ \ 1) \\ \hline 9\,635 \end{array}$$
  f
$$\begin{array}{r} 351 \\ \times\ 51 \\ \hline 17\,550\ (351 \times 50) \\ 351\ (351 \times\ \ 1) \\ \hline 17\,901 \end{array}$$

Challenge yourself
a 6110   **b** £13·44   **c** 3375

⑤ Times tables to 10 p10
1   18   49   56   16   18   54   36   42   21   9   45   40   80   54   24   40
    27   64   48   0   35   14   81   25   24   28   4   100   50   1   12   30
2   **a** 45   **b** 64   **c** 21   **d** 32   **e** 63   **f** 36   **g** 60   **h** 40
    i 56   **j** 18   **k** 16   **l** 48
3   **a** 5   **b** 9   **c** 2   **d** 8   **e** 7   **f** 8   **g** 10   **h** 8
    i 8   **j** 3   **k** 9   **l** 10

Challenge yourself
Answers will vary but include
a $4 \times 6 = 24$ **b** $6 \times 9 = 54$ **c** $6 \times 8 = 48$ **d** $7 \times 7 = 49$
e $1 \times 2 = 2$ **f** $9 \times 8 = 72$ **g** $6 \times 6 = 36$ **h** $2 \times 9 = 18$
i $3 \times 3 = 9$ **j** $7 \times 9 = 63$

⑥ Mode, median and mean p12
1   **a** Mode = 3, Median = 5
    b 1 1 1 2 3 4 6 6 7   Mode = 1, Median = 3
    c 2 2 2 3 5 5 6 7 9   Mode = 2, Median = 5
2   129 131 131 131 132 133 136 136 137 138 139
    Mode = 131, Median = 133

A2

---

3   4   **4** 43 kg
Challenge yourself
Answers will vary

⑦ Equivalent fractions p14
1   **b** $\frac{2}{4}$ $\frac{3}{6}$ $\frac{4}{8}$ $\frac{5}{10}$ $\frac{6}{12}$ **c** $\frac{2}{10}$ $\frac{3}{15}$ $\frac{4}{20}$ $\frac{5}{25}$ $\frac{6}{30}$
    d $\frac{2}{12}$ $\frac{3}{18}$ $\frac{4}{24}$ $\frac{5}{30}$ $\frac{6}{36}$ **e** $\frac{2}{20}$ $\frac{3}{30}$ $\frac{4}{40}$ $\frac{5}{50}$ $\frac{6}{60}$

2   **b** $5\frac{1}{3}$ **c** $5\frac{1}{4}$ **d** $5\frac{1}{9}$ **e** $4\frac{2}{7}$ **f** $8\frac{1}{2}$ **g** 4   **h** $3\frac{1}{8}$

3   Answers could include:
    a $\frac{3}{4}$ $\frac{6}{8}$ $\frac{12}{16}$ **b** $\frac{4}{14}$ $\frac{6}{21}$ $\frac{8}{28}$ **c** $\frac{2}{2}$ $\frac{3}{3}$ $\frac{4}{4}$
    d $\frac{22}{20}$ $\frac{33}{30}$ $\frac{44}{40}$ **e** $\frac{4}{10}$ $\frac{2}{5}$ $\frac{20}{50}$ **f** $\frac{1}{2}$ $\frac{2}{4}$ $\frac{12}{24}$

4   **a** $\frac{5}{20}$ **b** $\frac{1}{5}$ **c** $\frac{3}{4}$ **d** $\frac{18}{16}$

Challenge yourself
a $\frac{3}{4}$ **b** $\frac{1}{4}$ **c** $\frac{13}{100}$ **d** $\frac{1}{3}$

⑧ Decimals p16
1   **a** 8·32   **b** 2·601   **c** 13·19   **d** 6·054   **e** 22·81   **f** 5·55
2   **a** 3·34, 3·36, 3·38, 3·40   **b** 4·80, 4·85, 4·90, 4·95
3
$$\xleftarrow{\quad \overset{10·89}{\underset{10·9}{\downarrow}} \quad\quad \overset{10·99}{\underset{11·0}{\downarrow}} \quad\quad \underset{11·1}{} \quad\quad \overset{11·16}{\underset{11·2}{\downarrow}} \quad}$$
4   **a** 10 9 10   **b** 11 11 10   **c** 7 7 8   **d** 57 57 56
5   **a** 6·7   **b** 4·0   **c** 4·4   **d** 9·8   **e** 2·2   **f** 5·6

Challenge yourself
a   13·21   13·2   12·32   12·3   12·232   12·212
b   55·5   50·505   50·055   5·55   5·5   0·5

⑨ Co-ordinates p18
1   octagon

2   Answers will vary

Challenge yourself
a   (−5, −2), (−2, −2), (−5, −5), (−2, −5)
b   (2, 5), (5, 5), (2, 2), (5, 2)

How am I doing? p20
1   **a** even   **b** even   **c** odd   **d** even
2   **a** 8.0, 9.3, 10.6, 11.9   **b** 88, 71, 54, 37
3   **a** 7 615   **b** 5 117   **c** 216   **d** 451
4   **a** 2 000   **b** 7 014   **c** 2 000
5   **a** 21   **b** 7   **c** 6   **d** 63   **e** 5   **f** 4   **g** 9   **h** 8   **i** 9
6   **a** 5   **b** 7
7   **a** $\frac{2}{4}$ $\frac{3}{6}$ $\frac{4}{8}$ $\frac{5}{10}$ $\frac{6}{12}$ **b** $\frac{2}{10}$ $\frac{3}{15}$ $\frac{4}{20}$ $\frac{5}{25}$ $\frac{6}{30}$ **c** $\frac{2}{6}$ $\frac{3}{9}$ $\frac{4}{12}$ $\frac{5}{15}$ $\frac{6}{18}$
8   **a** 46   **b** 8   **c** 215
9   (1, −3), (1, 1), (−3, −3), (1, 1)

⑩ Negative numbers p22
1   **b** −18, −15, 2, 5, 20, 33   **c** −12, −2, 0, 1, 2, 12
    d −54, −36, −28, −21, −14, −12   **e** −14, −5, −1, 16, 21, 31
    f −303, −300, −30, −3, 30, 33   **g** −14, −7, 21, 38, 61, 62
2   **a** 4°C   **b** 0°C   **c** 15°C   **d** 21°C   **e** −8°C   **f** 29°C

⑪ Multiplication involving decimals p24

1 b $4 \times 4 = 16$ c $3 \times 8 = 24$ d $6 \times 2 = 12$
  e $10 \times 6 = 60$ f $1 \times 9 = 9$

2 a $4 \cdot 0 \times 4 = 16 \cdot 0$, $0 \cdot 9 \times 4 = 3 \cdot 6$, $19 \cdot 6$
  b $7 \cdot 0 \times 8 = 56 \cdot 0$, $0 \cdot 1 \times 8 = 0 \cdot 8$, $56 \cdot 8$
  c $3 \cdot 0 \times 2 = 6 \cdot 0$, $0 \cdot 6 \times 2 = 1 \cdot 2$, $7 \cdot 2$
  d $5 \cdot 0 \times 7 = 35 \cdot 0$, $0 \cdot 8 \times 7 = 5 \cdot 6$, $40 \cdot 6$
  e $1 \cdot 0 \times 9 = 9 \cdot 0$, $0 \cdot 9 \times 9 = 8 \cdot 1$, $17 \cdot 1$
  f $3 \cdot 0 \times 6 = 18 \cdot 0$, $0 \cdot 5 \times 6 = 3 \cdot 0$, $21 \cdot 0$

3 a $11 \cdot 8$ b $39 \cdot 6$ c $30 \cdot 6$

4 a $3 \cdot 00 \times 4 = 12 \cdot 00$, $0 \cdot 20 \times 4 = 0 \cdot 80$, $0 \cdot 01 \times 4 = 0 \cdot 04$, $12 \cdot 84$
  b $6 \cdot 00 \times 5 = 30 \cdot 00$, $0 \cdot 10 \times 5 = 0 \cdot 50$, $0 \cdot 09 \times 5 = 0 \cdot 45$, $30 \cdot 95$
  c $4 \cdot 00 \times 3 = 12 \cdot 00$, $0 \cdot 60 \times 3 = 1 \cdot 80$, $0 \cdot 07 \times 3 = 0 \cdot 21$, $14 \cdot 01$
  d $2 \cdot 00 \times 6 = 12 \cdot 00$, $0 \cdot 10 \times 6 = 0 \cdot 60$, $0 \cdot 08 \times 6 = 0 \cdot 48$, $13 \cdot 08$

a £48·75   b £51·75

⑫ Division p26

1 a 51   b 102   c 61   d 162   e 143   f 31 r1
  g 31 r1   h 71 r2   i 82   j 71 r4   k 91 r1   l 93 r1
  m 31   n 24 r3

2 a 20 r5   b 40 r7   c 20 r9

a 40 r7   b 20

⑬ Fractions of numbers p28

1 a 4   b 9   c 9   d 3   e 22   f 7   g 15   h 11

2 a 12   b 5   c 6   d 5   e 10   f 7   g 4   h 23
  i 9   j 8

3 a 10 20 40   b 18 60 90   c 9 30 45   d 20 14 22
  e 40 24 48

4 a $\frac{3}{5}$ b $\frac{1}{4}$ c $\frac{3}{10}$ d $\frac{1}{2}$ e $\frac{1}{3}$ f $\frac{1}{3}$ g $\frac{89}{100}$ h $\frac{1}{100}$

a $\frac{1}{3}$ b $\frac{1}{24}$ c $\frac{1}{8}$ d $\frac{1}{1440}$

⑭ Percentages p30

1 b 10%   c 50%   d 100%   e 1%   f 10%   g 50%
  h 25%   i 100%   j 1%

2 b 50%   c 6%   d 50%   e 70%   f 89%   g 46%
  h 100%   i 23%

3 b 25%   c 10%

4 e.g. a   b   c

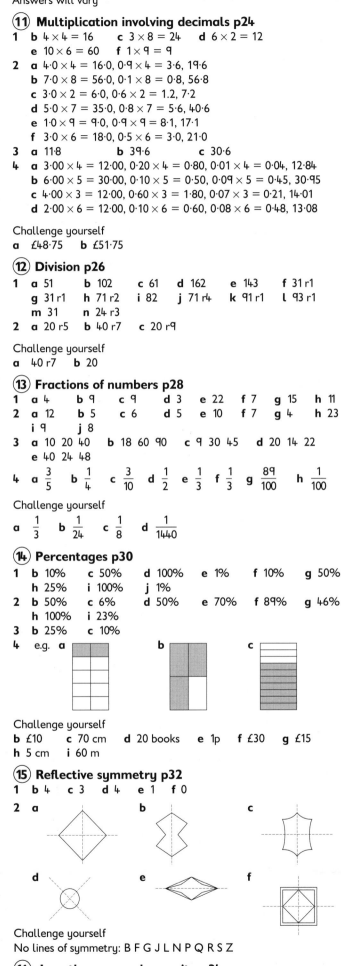

b £10   c 70 cm   d 20 books   e 1p   f £30   g £15
h 5 cm   i 60 m

⑮ Reflective symmetry p32

1 b 4   c 3   d 4   e 1   f 0

2 a   b   c

d   e   f

No lines of symmetry: B F G J L N P Q R S Z

⑯ Length, mass and capacity p34

1 a mm   b g   c m   d l   e g   f cm   g l   h g   i cm

2 Answers will vary

3 a 1·65 m or 165 cm   b 260 g   c 171 156 m

⑰ Solving problems p36

1 e.g. a $26 \div 15$ b 28×43
2 the money is in the biscuit tin

⑱ Line graphs p38

1

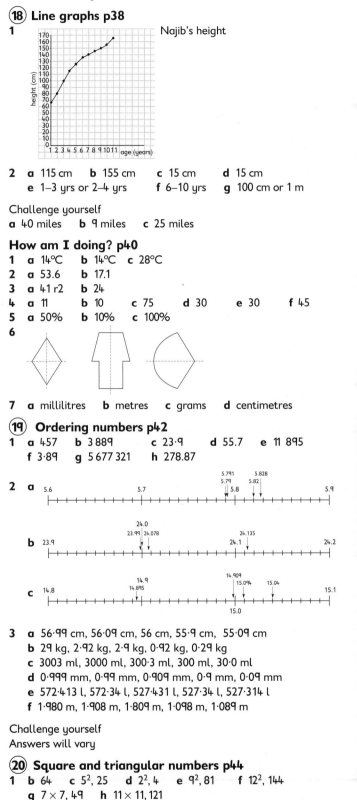

2 a 115 cm   b 155 cm   c 15 cm   d 15 cm
  e 1–3 yrs or 2–4 yrs   f 6–10 yrs   g 100 cm or 1 m

a 40 miles   b 9 miles   c 25 miles

How am I doing? p40

1 a 14°C   b 14°C   c 28°C
2 a 53.6   b 17.1
3 a 41 r2   b 24
4 a 11   b 10   c 75   d 30   e 30   f 45
5 a 50%   b 10%   c 100%
6

7 a millilitres   b metres   c grams   d centimetres

⑲ Ordering numbers p42

1 a 457   b 3 889   c 23·9   d 55.7   e 11 895
  f 3·89   g 5 677 321   h 278.87

2 a

b

c

3 a 56·99 cm, 56·09 cm, 56 cm, 55·9 cm, 55·09 cm
  b 29 kg, 2·92 kg, 2·9 kg, 0·92 kg, 0·29 kg
  c 3003 ml, 3000 ml, 300·3 ml, 300 ml, 30·0 ml
  d 0·999 mm, 0·99 mm, 0·909 mm, 0·9 mm, 0·09 mm
  e 572·413 l, 572·34 l, 527·431 l, 527·34 l, 527·314 l
  f 1·980 m, 1·908 m, 1·809 m, 1·098 m, 1·089 m

⑳ Square and triangular numbers p44

1 b 64   c 5^2, 25   d 2^2, 4   e 9^2, 81   f 12^2, 144
  g 7×7, 49   h 11×11, 121

2

1	4	9	16	25	36	49	64	81	100	121	144

3

1	3	6	10	15	21	28

4 The sequence of triangular numbers is built up by 1 (+2), 3 (+3), 6 (+4) 10 (+5) and so on.

169   45   120   225

21 Factors, multiples and prime numbers p46

1 a 2 5 10 **b** 4 5 10 **c** 9 2 18 **d** 1 2 31
e 9 3 27 6

2 a 36 78 60 **b** 81 117 36 **c** 60 144 84 **d** 49 28 105
e 15 215 90

3 Coloured numbers: 2, 3, 5, 7, 11, 13, 17, 19, 23, 29, 31, 37, 41, 43, 47, 53, 59, 61, 67, 71, 73, 79, 83, 89, 97

Challenge yourself
a coloured **b** 24th

22 Estimation p48

1 a 3000 **b** 85 **c** 550 **d** 8000 (approx.)

2 a 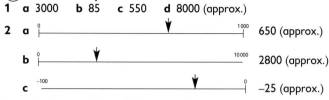 650 (approx.)

b 2800 (approx.)

c −25 (approx.)

3 a 50 (approx.) **b, c, d** Answers will vary

Challenge yourself
Spending one week on holiday, spending ten days in Spain and spending a fortnight skiing are all possible in the time given. Children may refer to having worked out how many days 1 300 000 seconds are equivalent to (15 days).

23 Ratio and proportion p50

1 b 1 to every 1 **c** 2 to every 3 **d** 1 to every 2
e 3 to every 2 **f** 2 to every 2 (or 1 to every 1)

2 b $\frac{1}{2}$ **c** $\frac{2}{5}$ **d** $\frac{1}{3}$ **e** $\frac{3}{5}$ **f** $\frac{2}{4}$ or $\frac{1}{2}$

3 a 12 girls **b** 6 cakes **c** 16 fish **d** 2 hours 20 minutes

Challenge yourself
The ratio of shape a to shape b is 3:1. The proportion of b's squares to the the the total number is $\frac{1}{4}$.

24 Area and perimeter p52

1 b P = 30 cm A = 36 cm² **c** P = 30 cm A = 56 cm²
2 a P = 28 cm A = 45 cm² **b** P = 40 cm A = 82 cm²
c P = 30 cm A = 42 cm²

Challenge yourself
a r = 50 cm² t = 25 cm² **b** r = 28 cm² t = 14 cm²
c r = 40 cm² t = 20 cm²

25 Angles p54

1 a obtuse **b** acute **c** acute **d** right angle
e obtuse **f** reflex

2 b  **c**
□ = obtuse
▨ = acute
■ = reflex

3 b 60° **c** 86° **d** 47° **e** 111°

Challenge yourself
a 304° **b** 225° **c** 349° **d** 105° **e** 162°

26 Shapes p56

1 a G **b** H **c** F **d** E
2 Answers will vary
3

circumference, diameter, radius

4 a kite **b** parallelogram **c** scalene triangle **d** trapezium

Challenge yourself
Answers will vary

27 Problems with money p58

1 a £53·44 **b** £36·50, £12·70, £18·90 **c** £11·55
d £60 506 **e** Answers will vary
f 10p, 20p, 26p, 30p, 36p, 46p, 52p, 56p, 62p, 72p, 78p, 82p, 88p, 98p, 108p

Challenge yourself
$7.20, €4.50

28 Probability p60

1 b certain **c** unlikely, possible **d** possible **e** impossible
f answers will vary **g** answers will vary

2 Answers will vary
3 Answers will vary

Challenge yourself
a $\frac{1}{6}$ **b** $\frac{1}{6}$ **c** $\frac{1}{6}$ **d** $\frac{1}{6}$

How am I doing? p62

1 3·03, 3·3, 3·303, 3·33, 3·333
2 Answers will vary but could include:
square numbers 25, 36, 49, 64, 81
triangular numbers 21, 28, 36, 45, 55
3 a 5, 3 **b** 15, 3, 5, 2, 6, 10 **c** 2, 7, 42, 12
4 a  28 (approx.)

b 650 (approx.)

c 2800 (approx.)

5 ratio = 3 black to every 4 white
proportion = $\frac{3}{7}$ black, $\frac{4}{7}$ white
6 P = 36 cm A = 68 cm² **7 a** 115° **b** 70°
8 Coloured shapes: E and F
9 Answers will vary

10–11 years Assessment p64

1 220.8
2 A prime number is only divisible by itself and 1.
Answers will vary but include: 3, 5, 7, 11, 13, 17
3 a 100% **b** 50%
4 Mode = 6 Median = 6
5 15°C **6** 22 **7** No **8** 29 **9** 28.8
10 Yes
11 $6\frac{2}{8}$ or $6\frac{1}{4}$
12 2.87, 2.78, 2.287, 2.278, 0.278
13 a 8.9 **b** 12.8 **c** 333.3
14 12 376

15 ✗

16
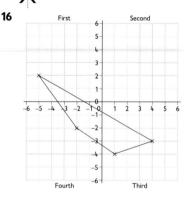
First, Second, Fourth, Third

17 Answers will vary
18 8
19 Answers will vary
20 24
21 a obtuse **b** reflex **c** acute
22 A = 37 cm² P = 26 cm
23
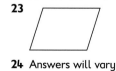

24 Answers will vary

2. Finish these shapes using the lines of symmetry shown.

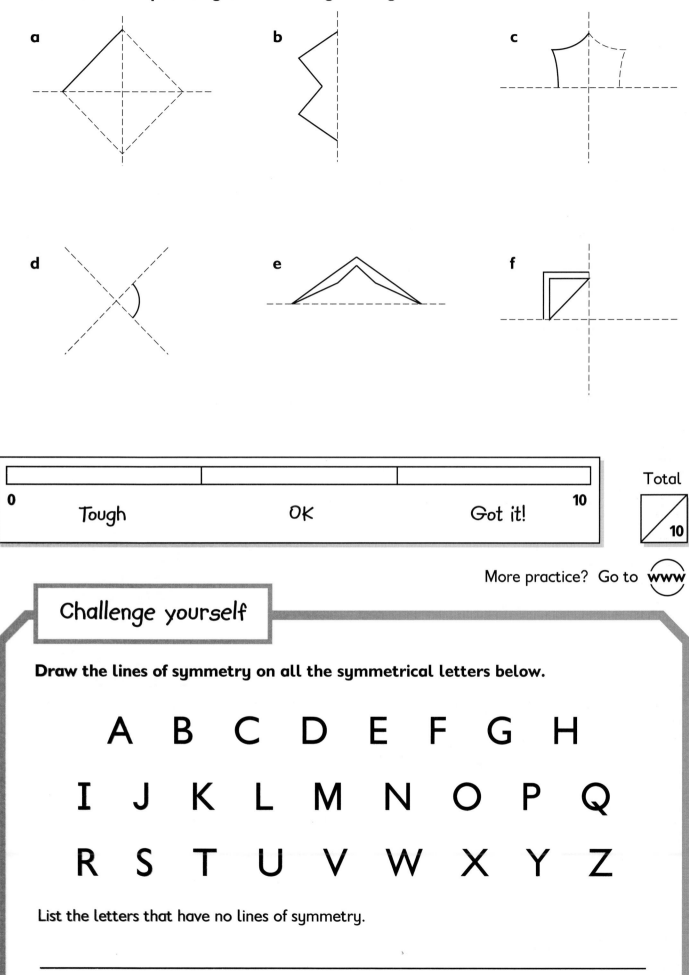

a

b

c

d

e

f

0		10
Tough	OK	Got it!

More practice? Go to www

Challenge yourself

Draw the lines of symmetry on all the symmetrical letters below.

A B C D E F G H

I J K L M N O P Q

R S T U V W X Y Z

List the letters that have no lines of symmetry.

_____

Length, mass and capacity

Standard metric units of measure for ...

Length	Mass	Capacity
millimetre (**mm**)	gram (**g**)	millilitre (**ml**)
centimetre (**cm**)	kilogram (**kg**)	centilitre (**cl**)
metre (**m**)	tonne	litre (**l**)
kilometre (**km**)		

1. **Which unit of measure would you use to measure ...**

   a the thickness of a rubber band? _____

   b the weight of an insect? _____

   c the depth of a swimming pool? _____

   d the contents of a bottle of lemonade? _____

   e the weight of a bag of crisps? _____

   f the width of a door? _____

   g the contents of an ice-cream container? _____

   h the weight of a toffee? _____

   i the length of a ruler? _____

2. **What could you measure using each of these units.**

   a a kilogram _____   b a tonne _____

   c a centilitre _____   d a centimetre _____

   e a gram _____   f a litre _____

3. **Solve these problems.**

a A group of friends made a daisy chain of 2·5 m. When they were holding it up to show their teacher, 85 cm broke away.

What length of the daisy chain was left? _____

b How many grams of sugar need to be added to 1·24 kg to make 1·5 kg altogether?

_____

c In an endurance competition, the first glider travelled 16·28 km, the second travelled 153·32 km and the third 1556 m.

How many metres did the three gliders travel altogether? _____

			Total
0 Tough	OK	Got it! 18	18

More practice? Go to www

Challenge yourself

Change this pancake recipe to approximate metric units.

Pancakes
~
9 oz flour

1 pint of milk

2 eggs

Pancakes
~
_____ g flour

_____ ml of milk

_____ eggs

Solving problems

Solving problems in maths is a way of playing with numbers.
Approach each problem as a challenge!

Calculators can help to speed up the process of finding the answer.

1. **Use a calculator to help you solve these problems.**

    a The answer is 1·7333333.
        Using two 2-digit whole numbers and a ÷ sign, write the number sentence with this answer.

    _____

    b The answer is 1204.
        Using two 2-digit whole numbers and a × sign, write the number sentence with this answer.

    _____

2. **You are a detective.**

You have been asked to crack the following code as quickly as possible to find the money!

You know each letter of the alphabet is a number between 1 and 9. The letters of the alphabet are numbered in order 1 to 9 and then repeated 1 to 9 until the alphabet is complete.

Crack the code.

285   46 557   91   95   285   2 913 392   295

Tough	OK	Got it!

0   3

More practice? Go to www

Total

3

Challenge yourself

Write a 'real life' number story for each of these calculations.

a $25.95 \times 15 = 389.25$

_____

_____

b $19.23 - 2.89 = 16.34$

_____

_____

Line graphs

Line graphs are used for continuous data, like the growth of a plant over three weeks or the changes in temperature over a month.

Lines join the points, clearly showing the changes made, usually over time.

1. **Draw a line graph to show the following data.**

Najib's height

age	1 yr	2 yrs	3 yrs	4 yrs	5 yrs	6 yrs	7 yrs	8 yrs	9 yrs	10 yrs	11 yrs
height	65 cm	80 cm	100 cm	115 cm	125 cm	135 cm	140 cm	145 cm	150 cm	155 cm	165 cm

Remember:
* to include three titles, one for each axis and one to explain the whole graph
* to decide what interval the height axis should increase by
* to join the dots neatly.

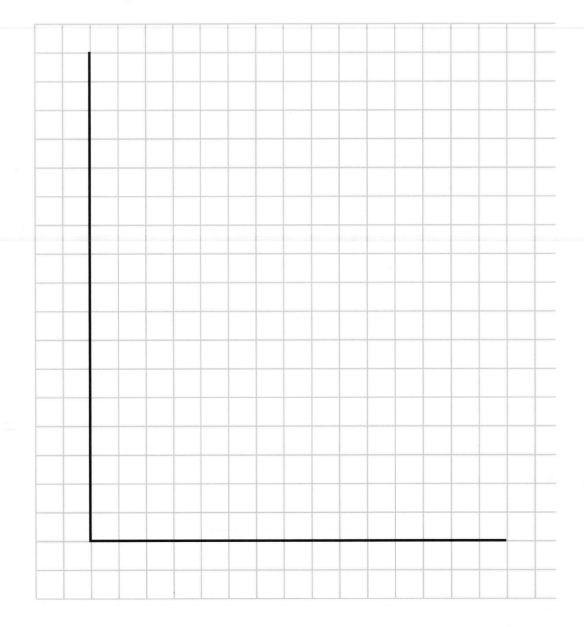

2. Look carefully at the graph you have drawn. Now answer these questions.

a What was Najib's height when he was 4? _____

b What was Najib's height when he was 10? _____

c Between the ages of 6 and 9 how much did Najib grow? _____

d Between the ages of 9 and 11 how much did Najib grow? _____

e In which 2-year period did Najib grow the fastest? _____

f Between which birthdays was Najib's growth constantly 5 cm a year? _____

g What is the increase in Najib's height between the years 1 and 11? _____

Tough	OK	Got it!

0   8

Total

/ 8

More practice? Go to www

More practice? Go to www

Challenge yourself

This sign shows distances in kilometres.
Using the conversion graph, re-write the sign in miles.

m

10 20 30 40 50 60 70 80
km

London	65 km
Reading	15 km
Oxford	40 km

a London _____ m

b Reading _____ m

c Oxford _____ m

How am I doing?

1.   **a**   The temperature is –8°C. How much must it rise to reach 6°C? _____

      b   The temperature is 11°C. How much must it drop to reach –3°C? _____

      c   The temperature is –14°C. How much must it rise to reach 14°C? _____

2.   **Find the answers to these number sentences.**

    a $6 \cdot 7 \times 8 =$ _____

    b $3 \cdot 42 \times 5 =$ _____

3.   **Work out the answers.**

    a $248 \div 6 =$ _____

    b $312 \div 13 =$ _____

4.   **What is...**

    a $\frac{1}{5}$ of 55? _____   **b** $\frac{2}{3}$ of 15? _____

    c $\frac{3}{4}$ of 100? _____   **d** $\frac{3}{7}$ of 70? _____

    e $\frac{5}{6}$ of 36? _____   **f** $\frac{9}{10}$ of 50? _____

5. Fill in the missing percentages.

a $\frac{1}{2}$ = _____ %

b 0.1 = _____ %

c 1 = _____ %

6. Draw the lines of reflective symmetry on these shapes.

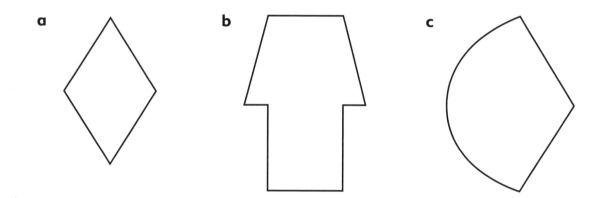

a

b

c

7. Join the dots to indicate which unit of measure you would use to measure …

a the contents of a mug   ●

b the height of a tree   ●

c the weight of 10 peas   ●

d the width of a calculator   ●

● grams

● metres

● centimetres

● millilitres

Total

23

More practice? Go to www

Ordering numbers

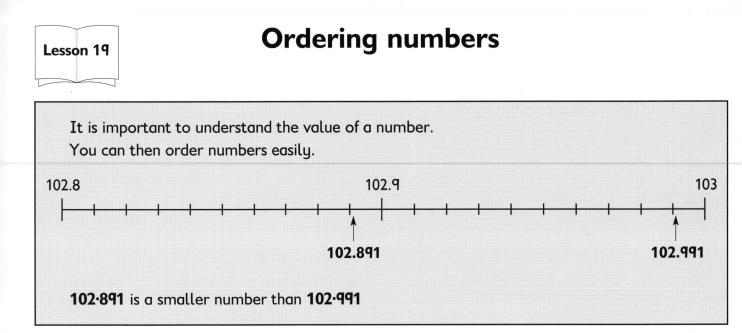

It is important to understand the value of a number.
You can then order numbers easily.

102.8   102.9   103

102.891   **102.991**

102·891 is a smaller number than **102·991**

1. **Look at these pairs of numbers.**
   Circle the smallest number.

   a 457   467   b 3890   3889

   c 23·9   29·3   d 56·7   55·7

   e 12 895   11 895   f 3·89   3·98

   g 5 678 321   5 677 321   h 279·87   278·87

2. **Place these decimals on the number line.**
   Use labelled arrows to show where they go.

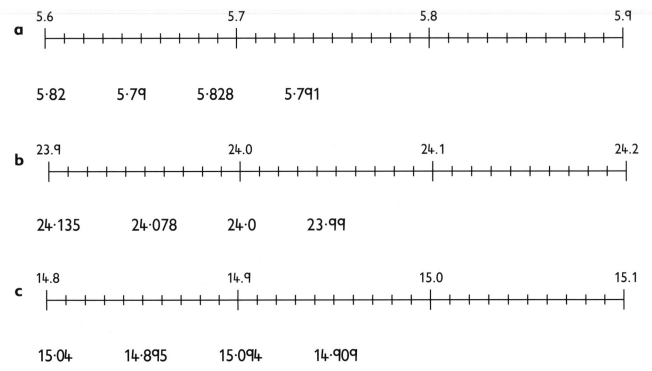

a   5.6   5.7   5.8   5.9

   5·82   5·79   5·828   5·791

b   23.9   24.0   24.1   24.2

   24·135   24·078   24·0   23·99

c   14.8   14.9   15.0   15.1

   15·04   14·895   15·094   14·909

3. **Order these measurements, largest first.**

a   56 cm   55·9 cm   56·99 cm   55·09 cm   56·09 cm

_____   _____   _____   _____   _____

b   2·9 kg   29 kg   0·29 kg   2·92 kg   0·92 kg

_____   _____   _____   _____   _____

c   300 ml   30·0 ml   3000 ml   300·3 ml   3003 ml

_____   _____   _____   _____   _____

d   0·99 mm   0·9 mm   0·999 mm   0·909 mm   0·09 mm

_____   _____   _____   _____   _____

e   572·34 l   527·34 l   527·314 l   572·413 l   527·431 l

_____   _____   _____   _____   _____

f   1·098 m   1·089 m   1·980 m   1·908 m   1·809 m

_____   _____   _____   _____   _____

| 0 | Tough | OK | Got it! | 17 |

More practice? Go to www

Total
17

Challenge yourself

Between the numbers provided, write three more numbers in order.

a   467·3   [ ]   [ ]   [ ]   467·4

b   2 314 556   [ ]   [ ]   [ ]   2 314 550

c   7·98   [ ]   [ ]   [ ]   7·986

d   312·67   [ ]   [ ]   [ ]   312·68

e   1·1   [ ]   [ ]   [ ]   1·15

f   466 723.009   [ ]   [ ]   [ ]   466 723.1

<table>
<tr><td style="border:1px solid;padding:10px;">Lesson 20</td></tr>
</table>

Square and triangular numbers

A **square number** is a number multiplied by itself.

It looks like a square!

$$4 \times 4 = \boxed{} = 4^2 = 16$$

1. **Fill in the gaps.**

    a $6 \times 6 =$ ___6^2___ = ___36___

    b $8 \times 8 =$ ___8^2___ = _____

    c $5 \times 5 =$ _____ = _____

    d $2 \times 2 =$ _____ = _____

    e $9 \times 9 =$ _____ = _____

    f 12×12 _____ = _____

    g _____ $= 7^2 =$ _____

    h _____ $= 11^2 =$ _____

2. **Complete this number sequence of square numbers.**

1			16			49			100		

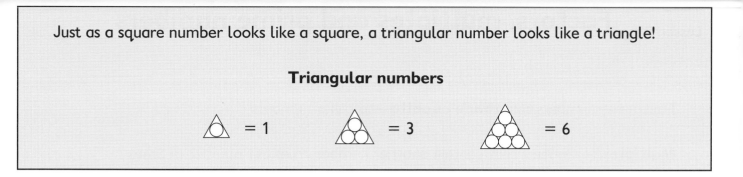

Just as a square number looks like a square, a triangular number looks like a triangle!

Triangular numbers

= 1   = 3   = 6

3. **Find the next four triangular numbers.**

1	3	6				

4. **Write a rule for finding triangular numbers.**

_____

_____

0	Tough	OK	Got it!	11

Total

11

More practice? Go to www

Challenge yourself

Look at the numbers below. They are either square or triangular numbers.
Draw a triangle or square around each number to show which category they
belong to.

169   45   120   225

Factors, multiples and prime numbers

Factors = numbers that **divide equally** into other numbers

Multiples = numbers that contain another number an **exact** number of times

1. **Ring the numbers in the box that are factors of ...**

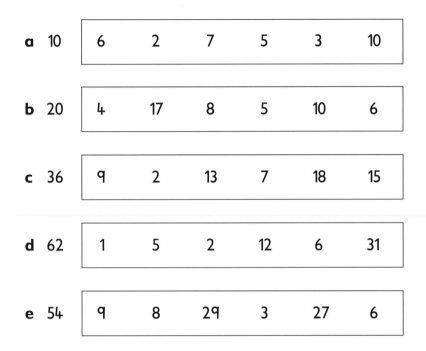

a 10 | 6   2   7   5   3   10

b 20 | 4   17   8   5   10   6

c 36 | 9   2   13   7   18   15

d 62 | 1   5   2   12   6   31

e 54 | 9   8   29   3   27   6

2. **Ring the numbers in the box that are multiples of ...**

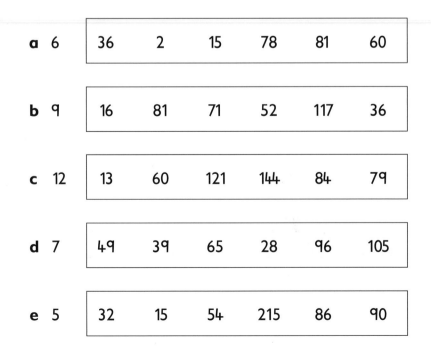

a 6 | 36   2   15   78   81   60

b 9 | 16   81   71   52   117   36

c 12 | 13   60   121   144   84   79

d 7 | 49   39   65   28   96   105

e 5 | 32   15   54   215   86   90

A **prime number** has only two factors:

1 and the number itself.

QUICK TIP!
1 is not a prime number as it only has one factor!

3. **On the 10 × 10 square, colour in all the prime numbers.**
   The first two have been done for you.

0	1	2	3	4	5	6	7	8	9
10	11	12	13	14	15	16	17	18	19
20	21	22	23	24	25	26	27	28	29
30	31	32	33	34	35	36	37	38	39
40	41	42	43	44	45	46	47	48	49
50	51	52	53	54	55	56	57	58	59
60	61	62	63	64	65	66	67	68	69
70	71	72	73	74	75	76	77	78	79
80	81	82	83	84	85	86	87	88	89
90	91	92	93	94	95	96	97	98	99

0	Tough	OK	Got it! 11

Total

11

More practice? Go to www

Challenge yourself

A line of counters is set out in a pattern.

2 white   3 coloured   2 white   3 coloured . . .

○○●●●○○●●●○○●●●○○●

a   Is the 48th counter white or coloured? _____

b   What position in the line is the 14th coloured counter? _____

Estimation

Estimate = guess the nearest

0   ↓   1 000

Estimation ≈ 750

Remember to look carefully at the scale of the line.

1. **Estimate the number that the arrow is pointing to.**

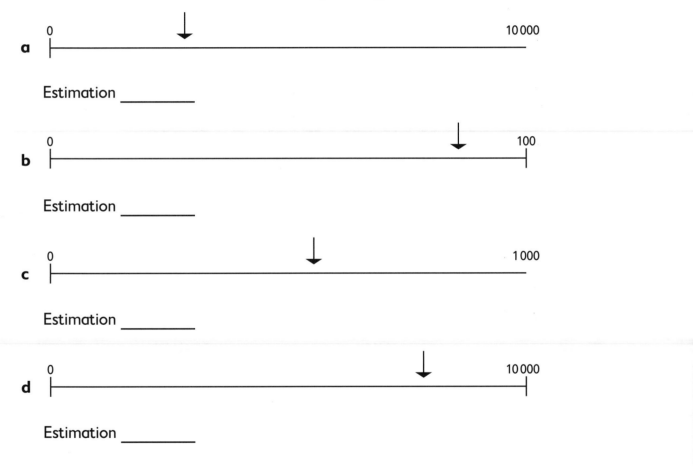

a

0   ↓   10 000

Estimation _____

b

0   ↓   100

Estimation _____

c

0   ↓   1 000

Estimation _____

d

0   ↓   10 000

Estimation _____

2. **Draw an arrow where you estimate these numbers will be on each of the number lines.**

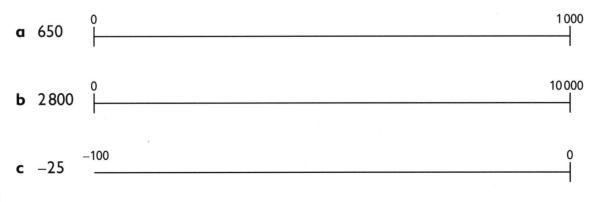

a 650   0   1 000

b 2 800   0   10 000

c −25   −100   0

3. **Estimate the right answer to these problems.**

Show your workings. Use ≈ in your workings.

QUICK TIP!
≈ is the same as writing 'is approximately equal to'

a Estimate how many penny coins will make a straight line 1 m long. _____

b Estimate how many bricks there are in a wall of your house. _____

c Estimate how many loaves of bread your family will eat during 10 years. _____

d Estimate how many leaves are on a tree near your house. _____

0	Tough	OK	Got it!	11

Total

11

More practice? Go to www

Challenge yourself

If you had 1 300 000 seconds, which of these would you be able to do?

- spend one week on holiday

- spend ten days in Spain

- spend a fortnight skiing

- spend a month on a holiday cruise

- spend a year going around the world

Explain how you decided.

_____

_____

Ratio and proportion

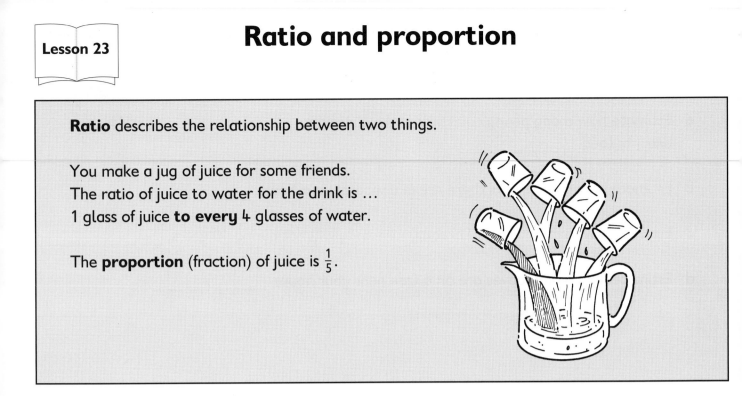

Ratio describes the relationship between two things.

You make a jug of juice for some friends.
The ratio of juice to water for the drink is …
1 glass of juice **to every** 4 glasses of water.

The **proportion** (fraction) of juice is $\frac{1}{5}$.

1. **Write the ratio of black squares to white squares in each of these patterns.**

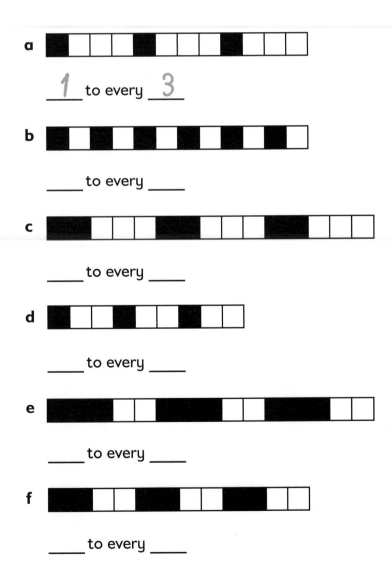

a

___1___ to every ___3___

b

_____ to every _____

c

_____ to every _____

d

_____ to every _____

e

_____ to every _____

f

_____ to every _____

2. **Now write the number of black squares as a fraction of the total in each of the patterns in 1.**

a ___$\frac{1}{4}$___

b _____

c _____

d _____

e _____

f _____

3. **Solve these problems.**

a There are two girls for every three boys watching a school football match.
30 children are watching the match.

How many girls are watching? _____

b There is a plate of 24 cakes. Caleb eats one in every four cakes.

How many cakes does he eat? _____

c Mr Bevan has 40 fish in his pond. A stork eats two in every five of his fish.

How many fish does the stork eat? _____

d A joint of beef needs to be cooked for 40 minutes for every kg.

How long does a $3\frac{1}{2}$ kg joint of beef take to cook? _____

0			14
Tough	OK	Got it!	

Total

14

More practice? Go to www

Challenge yourself

Look at these shapes.
Describe in terms of ratio and proportion
the relationship between the two shapes.

_____

_____

_____

Perimeter and area

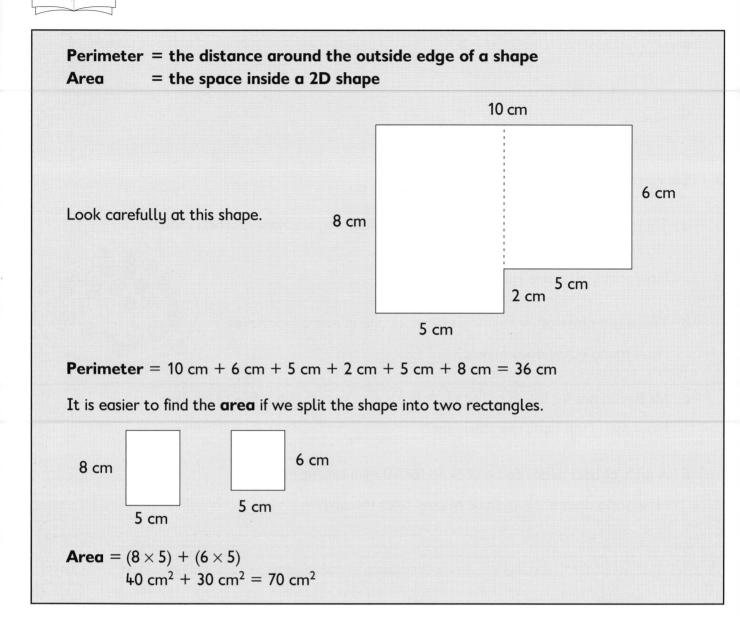

Perimeter = the distance around the outside edge of a shape
Area = the space inside a 2D shape

Look carefully at this shape.

10 cm

8 cm

6 cm

5 cm

2 cm

5 cm

5 cm

Perimeter = 10 cm + 6 cm + 5 cm + 2 cm + 5 cm + 8 cm = 36 cm

It is easier to find the **area** if we split the shape into two rectangles.

8 cm

5 cm

6 cm

5 cm

Area = $(8 \times 5) + (6 \times 5)$
40 cm^2 + 30 cm^2 = 70 cm^2

1. **Find the perimeter and the area of these rectangles.**

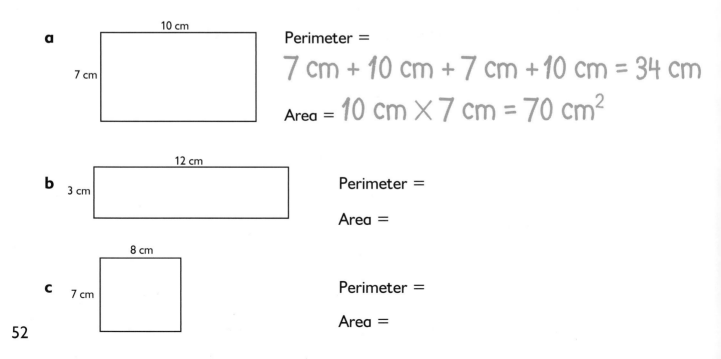

a

10 cm

7 cm

Perimeter =

7 cm + 10 cm + 7 cm + 10 cm = 34 cm

Area = 10 cm × 7 cm = 70 cm^2

b 3 cm

12 cm

Perimeter =

Area =

c 7 cm

8 cm

Perimeter =

Area =

2. **Find the perimeter and area of these shapes.**

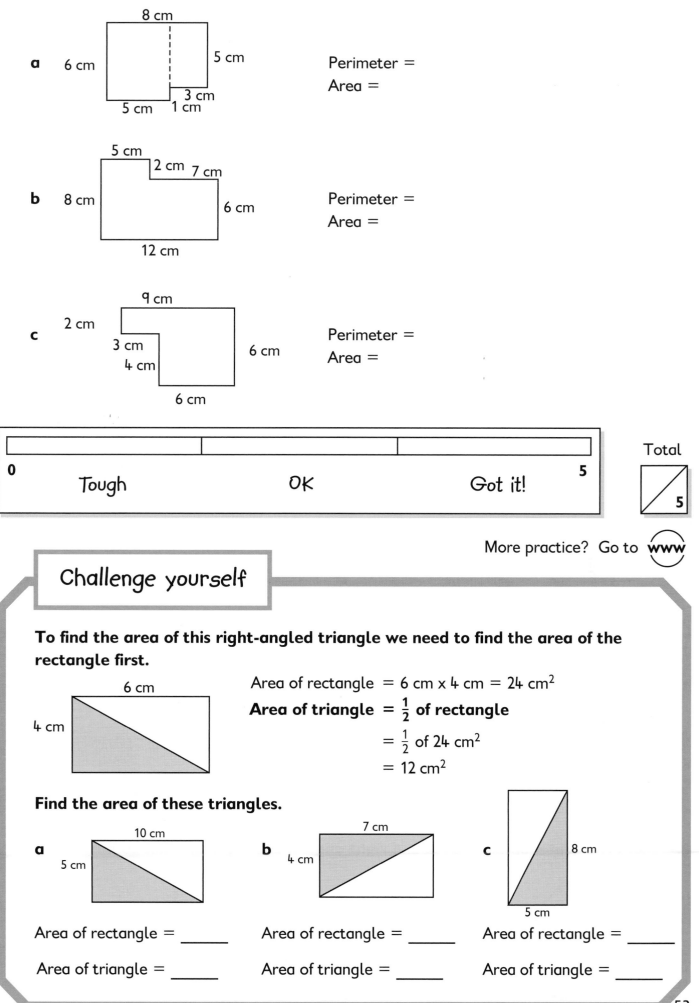

a   8 cm
     6 cm   5 cm   Perimeter =
        5 cm   3 cm   Area =
               1 cm

b   5 cm
        2 cm 7 cm
     8 cm   6 cm   Perimeter =
          12 cm   Area =

c   9 cm
     2 cm
        3 cm   6 cm   Perimeter =
        4 cm   Area =
          6 cm

0			5
Tough	OK	Got it!	

Total

5

More practice? Go to www

Challenge yourself

To find the area of this right-angled triangle we need to find the area of the rectangle first.

6 cm

4 cm

Area of rectangle = 6 cm x 4 cm = 24 cm²
Area of triangle = $\frac{1}{2}$ of rectangle
                    = $\frac{1}{2}$ of 24 cm²
                    = 12 cm²

Find the area of these triangles.

a   10 cm
     5 cm

b   7 cm
     4 cm

c   8 cm
        5 cm

Area of rectangle = _____

Area of triangle = _____

Area of rectangle = _____

Area of triangle = _____

Area of rectangle = _____

Area of triangle = _____

Angles

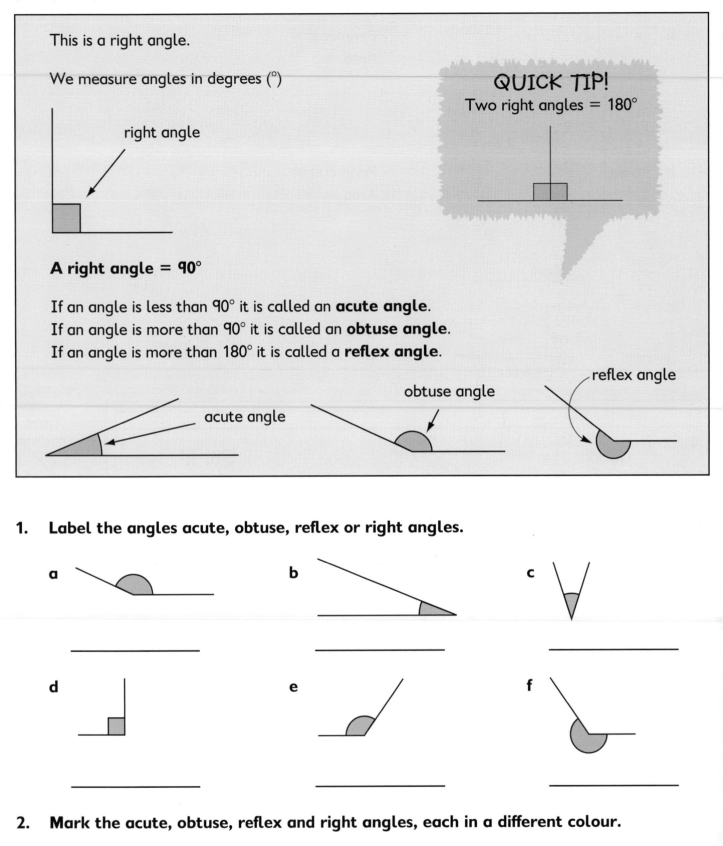

This is a right angle.

We measure angles in degrees (°)

right angle

QUICK TIP!
Two right angles = 180°

A right angle = 90°

If an angle is less than 90° it is called an **acute angle**.
If an angle is more than 90° it is called an **obtuse angle**.
If an angle is more than 180° it is called a **reflex angle**.

reflex angle

obtuse angle

acute angle

1. **Label the angles acute, obtuse, reflex or right angles.**

a   b   c

_____   _____   _____

d   e   f

_____   _____   _____

2. **Mark the acute, obtuse, reflex and right angles, each in a different colour.**

a   b   c

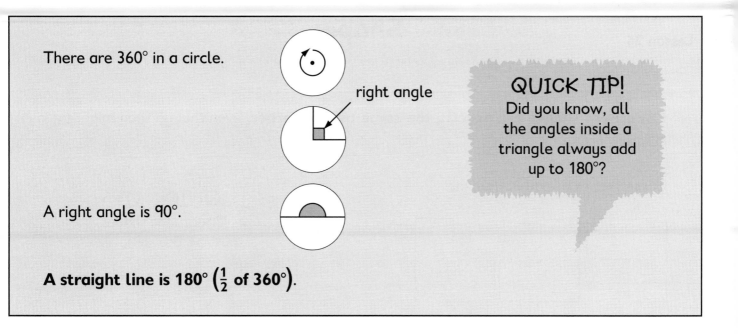

There are 360° in a circle.

right angle

QUICK TIP!
Did you know, all the angles inside a triangle always add up to 180°?

A right angle is 90°.

A straight line is 180° ($\frac{1}{2}$ of 360°).

3. **Match the angles, so the two angles joined together will make a straight line (180°).**

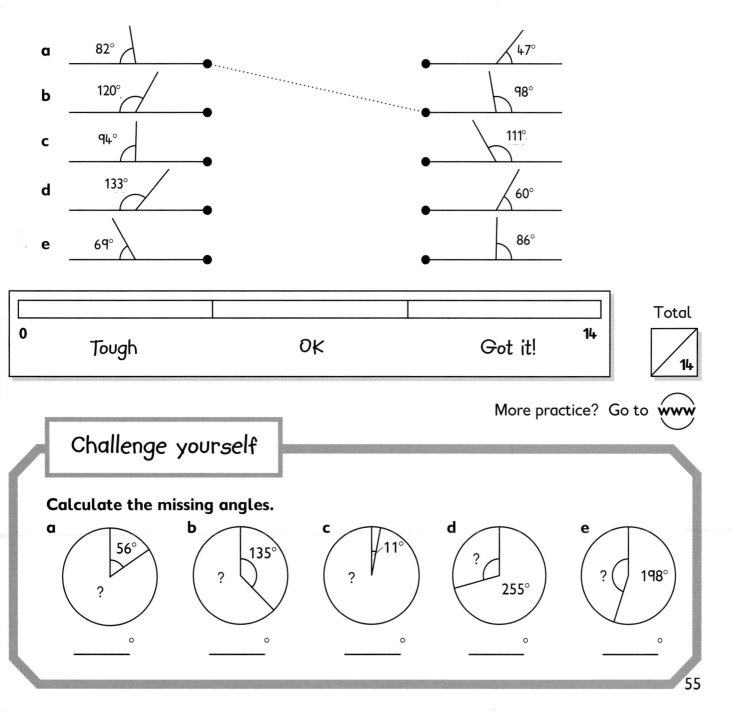

a   82°

b   120°

c   94°

d   133°

e   69°

47°

98°

111°

60°

86°

Tough	OK	Got it!

0

14

Total

14

More practice? Go to **www**

Challenge yourself

Calculate the missing angles.

a   56°   ?

b   135°   ?

c   11°   ?

d   ?   255°

e   ?   198°

_____ °   _____ °   _____ °   _____ °   _____ °

Shapes

Congruent shapes are exactly the same as each other, even though they might be in different positions.

These shapes are all congruent.

QUICK TIP!
Congruent shapes
must be the same size.

The shape is exactly the same, although it looks different because it has been turned.

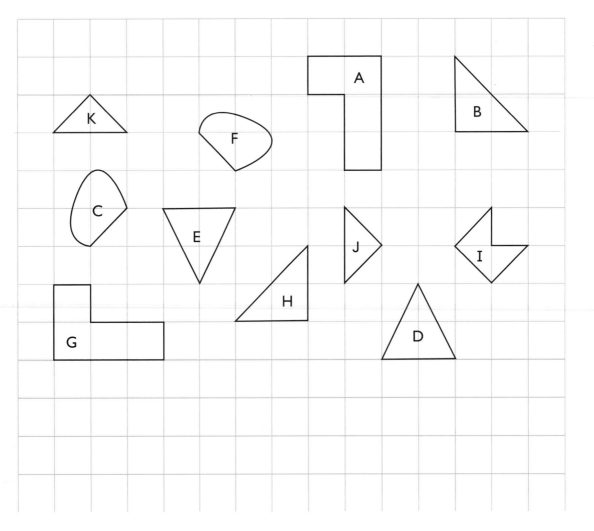

1. **Which shape is congruent with ...**

   a A? _____   **b** B? _____   **c** C? _____   **d** D? _____

2. **In the space available above, draw a different congruent shape for A and another for B.**

All these definitions are labels of measure for a circle.

radius = the distance from the centre of a circle to any point on the circumference
diameter = the distance across a circle, through the centre
circumference = the perimeter of a circle

3. **Label the radius, diameter and circumference on this circle.**

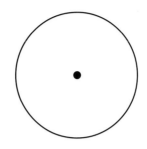

4. **With a line, match each of these 2D shapes with its name.**

a

b

c

d

scalene triangle   trapezium   kite   parallelogram

0   Tough   OK   Got it!   **10**

Total

/10

More practice? Go to www

Challenge yourself

Write a description for each of the shapes in question 4, without naming the shape.

a kite _____

b trapezium _____

c scalene triangle _____

d parallelogram _____

Check your definitions in a dictionary.
Now, without giving away the name of the shape, read your description to someone.
Can they name the shape?

Problems with money

Often, without realising it, we solve problems with money.

When you choose a packet of sweets to buy, do you ever wonder if you have enough money left to buy a few more?

Before attempting a money problem, think carefully about the operation or operations (+, −, ×, ÷) you need to use to solve it.

1. **Solve the following problems.**

   a Tuhil's mum bought him a pair of trousers that cost £15·99, a jumper for £12·50 and a new pair of shoes for £24·95.

   How much money did she spend? _____

   b What was the price of these items before the sale?

   Tennis racket _____

   Hockey stick _____

   Football _____

   c If a packet of stickers cost 55p, how much would 21 packets cost? _____

d Six people won £363 036 between them on the lottery.

How much did each person get? _____

e You have £1 worth of coins.
(4 x 1p, 3 x 2p, 4 x 5p, 3 x 10p, 2 x 20p)
Can you find at least ten different ways of using the coins to pay 45p exactly?

f You have three 26p stamps and three 10p stamps.
Find all the different amounts you could stick on a parcel.

Tough	OK	Got it!

0   6

Total

/ 6

More practice? Go to www

Challenge yourself

Converting to foreign currency.

The exchange rates for £1 are:

> **Bureau de change**
>
> $2.40 Australian dollars
> €1.50 euros

QUICK TIP!
Exchange rate for £1 = how much foreign currency you would get for a pound.

How many dollars and euros do you get for £3?

dollars _____   euros _____

Probability

Probability is the likelihood of something happening.

1. **Match the statements with the boxes. Some may link with more than one box.**

a I will eat breakfast in the morning ●   ● CERTAIN

b It will get dark at night ●

      ● LIKELY

c I will see the Queen tomorrow ●

d It will rain on my birthday ●   ● UNLIKELY

e I will stand on the moon next week ●

      ● IMPOSSIBLE

f I will eat a bag of crisps at the weekend ●

g I will talk to a friend tonight ●   ● POSSIBLE

2. **Read the example and list two more events that can have only two possible outcomes.**

The new baby will be a boy or a girl.

_____

_____

3. **List two events that have only one possible outcome.**

_____

_____

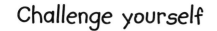
Challenge yourself

Answer the questions below by conducting your own experiment.

How many times do you need to throw a dice to get a 6?

Make a note of the number of times you need to throw a dice to get a 6.
Do this 15 times.

Fill in the table.

Experiment	No of throws to get a 6
1	
2	
3	
4	
5	
6	
7	
8	
9	
10	
11	
12	
13	
14	
15	

Look at the table above.

What is the probability of throwing a 6 …

a on the first throw? _____

b on the third throw? _____

c on the sixth throw? _____

d on the tenth throw? _____

How am I doing?

1. **Order these numbers, smallest first.**

   3·33   3·303   3·3   3·333   3·03

   _____   _____   _____   _____   _____

2. **Write two square and two triangular numbers greater than the number 17.**

   square numbers

   triangular numbers

3. **Ring the numbers in the box that are factors of ...**

   a 15

   | 7 | 11 | 5 | 14 | 3 | 21 |

   b 30

   | 15 | 3 | 5 | 2 | 6 | 10 |

   c 84

   | 2 | 10 | 7 | 42 | 12 | 15 |

4. **Draw an arrow where you estimate the number will be on the number line.**

   a 28
   0 ————————————————————————————————— 100

   b 650
   0 ————————————————————————————————— 1000

   c 2 800
   0 ————————————————————————————————— 10 000

5. **Write the ratio and proportion of black squares to white squares.**

   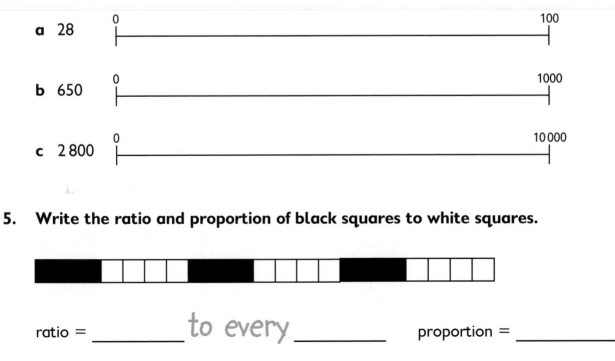

   ratio = _____ to every _____   proportion = _____

62

6. Find the perimeter and area of this shape.

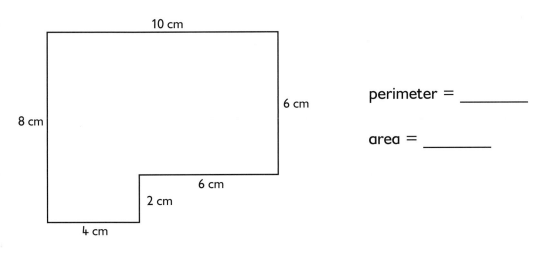

perimeter = _____

area = _____

7. Fill in the missing angle:

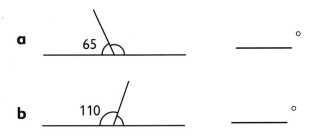

a   65   _____ °

b   110   _____ °

8. Colour the shapes that are congruent with A.

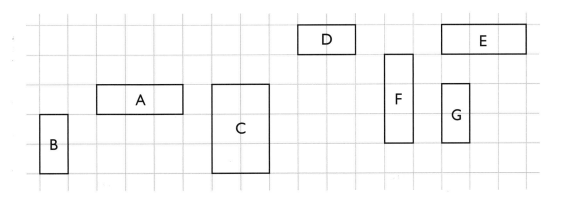

9. Write a statement where the probability of something happening is **UNLIKELY**.

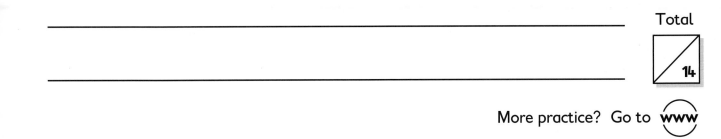

_____   Total

_____

14

More practice? Go to www

10–11 Years Assessment

1. Find the total of 32·6, 63·2 and 125. _____

2. What is a prime number?

   _____

3. Write the percentage.   **a** 1·0 = _____%   **b** 0·5 = _____%

4. Write the mode and median of these numbers.

   6   7   1   3   9   6   1   2   6

   Mode = _____   Median = _____

5. The temperature is –7°C. How much does it rise to reach 8°C? _____

6. Divide 506 by 23. _____

7. Look at the number sentences. The first is correct; is the second?

   $36 \times 45 = 1620$ $1620 \div 45 = 37$ [   ]

8. How many eighths in $3\frac{5}{8}$? _____

9. Complete this number sentence. $4·8 \times 6 =$ _____

10. Is 462 divisible by 3?   Yes   /   No

11. Change this improper fraction to a mixed number. $\frac{50}{8} =$ _____

12. Put these numbers in order, largest first.

    2·78   2·87   0·278   2·278   2·287

    _____   _____   _____   _____   _____

13. Write the following to one decimal place.

    a 8·92 _____   **b** 12·831 _____   **c** 333·333 _____

14. Multiply 442 by 28. _____

15. Draw all the lines of symmetry on this letter.   **X**